Back to the Beginning

Judy Andrews

Back to the Beginning

Remarkable True Stories of Adoption Searches & Reunions

From the Case Files of Research Etc.

RESEARCH ETC., Inc.
Scottsdale, Arizona

Ava Friddle, Judy Andrews, Kristen Hamilton

PRIVATE INVESTIGATORS

with Joe Bardin

RESEARCH ETC., Inc.
Scottsdale, Arizona

Research Etc., Inc.
8390 E. Via De Ventura, #F110-184
Scottsdale, AZ 85260
Tel: (480) 664-4345
Fax: (480) 367-0119
www.backtothebeginningbook.com

Printed in the United States of America

ISBN13: 978-0-9816412-0-1
ISBN10: 0-9816412-0-2

FIRST EDITION 2008

Graphic Design Assistance by Keith Andrews

Dedicated to the loving memory of

Vesta Jo Hefley Ewing

whose lifelong love of books was handed down
to all of her children and grandchildren.

Endless Dream

So near and yet so far
The space of time
The expanse of space
Since last I saw your face.

It haunts me day and night
This endless dream
That you are real
The truth I cannot feel.

The hopeful cord of life
Gives witness to our cause
Your presence will at last declare
What likenesses we share.

Look up to light
Reach out to hope
The journey's been so long
Come, let freedom be our song.

—Rachel Smith,
Birthmother

Contents

Acknowledgments

Our sincere gratitude goes out to each and every adoptee, birthparent, adoptive parent, sibling, cousin, aunt, uncle and friend who opened their souls and contributed their heartfelt thoughts to the pages of this book.

We deeply appreciate the encouragement of our family and our large extended family that have all waited patiently for this book to finally come to fruition.

A special thank you to Lance F. Jacobs, Esq., our mentor and dear friend, for the invaluable insight and support he always provides.

And last, but not least, thank you, Joe Bardin, for spending many long hours listening to our stories and for being as inspired by them as we have been.

Introduction

Secrecy breeds mystery. The big myth among many adoptees is that everyone's birthmother is either a rape-victim, a prostitute, or a movie-star. Such dramatic assumptions come from the secrecy that shrouds the adoption process. It's human nature to assume that if something is hidden from us, there are reasons for this, and that those reasons are much more spectacular than we dare believe. It's also human nature to want to know the truth.

This is not a book of 'advice' or 'how-to'—it is a collection of stories from our case files. We wrote this book to illustrate how every search and reunion is unique to each individual.

It is our most sincere hope that our readers will enjoy this collection of short stories and that some light may be shed on what was once, and sometimes still is, such a mysterious subject. We love what we do and we are blessed to be able to help people find answers to very important questions about their beginnings. We have been enriched beyond measure by the friendships of the many wonderful people we have worked with.

These are true stories, published with permission from our clients and their family members. We have changed the names, places and some minor events to protect the identities of our clients, because, as always, we remain '*Strictly Confidential!*'

CHAPTER 1

A Family Affair

Our Beginning as an Agency

Research Etc, Inc. was founded in 1995, and is the product of a collective brainstorm between sisters Kristen Hamilton and Judy Andrews, along with their mother Ava Friddle. Through Research Etc., they have conducted more than 500 adoption searches and have successfully resolved approximately 98% of them.

From the beginning, it's been a family affair. Kristen, who was a paralegal, was also a first time expectant mother and starting a family-owned business would give her the opportunity to continue working while being at home with her child. At the same time, it would allow Ava and Judy a hand in raising this eagerly awaited baby, the first in their family in eighteen years.

Searching for and reuniting with old friends & lost loves, etc. had become very popular and widespread, and since we were all pretty much computer literate along with being just plain nosy, this type of business seemed to be our most natural course of action. With Kristen's paralegal background and her gift of gab, Judy's land records expertise along with her limitless tenacity, and Ava's many years of office management (plus, she says raising two daughters made her a natural detective), the investigation field seemed the logical choice for an interesting and rewarding family-based business.

Once decided upon, we went to work. We were lucky in that Ava had a large, empty sunroom in her home that we could use for an office and we quickly installed new telephones, office machines and furniture. Business cards were ordered and although we already had a large collection of software to help with our searches, we bought more.

We agreed on the name *Research Etc.* for our agency because we thought it sounded honest and non-threatening, and that's what we wanted our business to be.

Our next step was to call on Judy's daughter Amy and her boyfriend Shawn, both college students, to design and maintain a website for us. We advertised as being 'People-Finders,' searching for and reuniting 'old classmates, lost loves, military buddies,' etc. As soon as our website appeared on the computer, our phones started ringing and we were in business! Or so we thought.

Stop! In The Name Of The Law

All during our preparations, Kristen's husband, who is an Arizona Department of Public Safety Officer, kept trying to tell us we couldn't just jump up and start that type of business without obtaining a license, but we were too excited and busy to listen and we just kept ignoring him; until the day he brought us to a screeching halt! He came into our office, carrying a huge Arizona State Statutes book, and *commanded* the three of us to 'sit down and listen' while he read the facts to us. The one fact that really made us sit up and pay attention was that we could *go to jail* if we didn't obtain the proper license for this sort of work. That really took the wind out of our sails—but not for long.

We applied for an Arizona Private Investigation license and after a long application and verification process, we met all the legal requirements, and our license was issued. Kristen, with her paralegal background, was the qualifying agent and Judy and Ava were named as Associates. By May of that year, we were in business. Legally.

When we obtained our license, we couldn't, without a guilty conscience, leave out Judy's daughter Amy Andrews[1], who was also named as an Associate. Our newest partner, six month old Kelsey, (Kristen's daughter, Judy's niece and Ava's granddaughter), was happily installed in a playpen in the center of everyone and everything. We called her our 'Pee-Pee I' and, contently swinging from one of our hips to another, she was a detective before she could even talk.

The Search Of Their Lives

After obtaining our license many private search resources became open to us, and we soon were very successful in our field. Kristen entered a program for Confidential Intermediaries through the Arizona Supreme Court and we added 'adoption searches' to our list of services. It is a very rewarding part of our business and it is those cases that bring us eagerly to the office each morning and keep us going until late in the night. Each and every case is different and brings with it new challenges and learning experiences for us.

Anyone that becomes involved in adoption searches soon becomes aware of the term 'adoption triad' which relates to the three core members of an adoption: Birthparent, Adoptee, and the Adoptive Parents. Since no one at Research Etc. is an adoptee, or an adoptive mother, nor have we ever relinquished a child for adoption, we are often asked:

---

1 From the age of four years, all that Amy ever wanted to be when she grew up was a detective, sort of like Dick Tracy. She spent all of her allowance on detective magazines, mail order badges, handcuffs, spyglasses, fingerprint kits and other detective paraphernalia. We all laughed at her and told her that in no way would that ever happen. Although Amy is still a partner and helps with the websites, she is now pursuing a career in International Marketing and, although she is not active in our investigation work, she is officially a detective.

> "Why do you feel qualified to do this work if you are not a triad member? And how can you relate to the issues that surround triad members?"

Kristen answers the questions this way:

> "I was not adopted, therefore, there is no mystery surrounding how I came to be and where I come from. I have extended family members and close friends that are adoptive parents, and I know their feelings and the joy that their children bring into our family circle. I have never had to experience carrying a child for nine months and then handing it over to strangers. But I can imagine the immense pain, frustration, fear and utter infuriation I would feel if I were denied the basic knowledge about something that so personally involved me.
>
> "I walk into my office every day hoping I can help fill in the blanks in a client's life. I am personally gratified when I help someone find the answers that have been denied him or her for all their lives—answers to questions that most people take for granted. I have talked with, and cried with, so many adoptees, birthparents and adoptive parents and have felt their pain and their joy. Strangely enough, although I am only a voice on a phone, I am often the only person whom they have ever spoken openly with about their fears and sorrow. Along with my investigative experience, it is my compassion for others that qualifies me to do this work. I also have a little stubborn streak and never give up on a search. That helps, too!"

Our Search Philosophy

Adoption investigations are a specialty completely different from others. One must understand how the court system works now *and how it previously worked* in the given year that the adoption took place. They must determine what records may exist, what resources are available—and where to go find them. The adoption investigator is usually looking for someone whose name is completely unknown. It is an understatement to say that it is a challenge to try to sift through the billions of women in the world to find *'a girl with brown hair and brown eyes, who loves to sew and listen to music.'* Often that is the only information the adoption investigator may have to work with.

Occasionally there are rare and miraculous cases where an error was made, either forty years ago or currently, and a paper is given to someone with a name and other identifying information. Those cases are uncommon blessings. Generally, for the investigator, the search becomes like a jigsaw puzzle. Each piece must fit before the birthparent or adoptee is identified and located.

Searching The Internet

The numerous adoption registries that are posted on the Internet can produce positive search results, but searching for a birthparent or adult adoptee online can be like searching for a needle in a haystack. Back in 1995, when our agency was new, the Internet had very limited capabilities. Over the years it has grown and is now a powerful tool for the private investigator—mainly because it has allowed companies to provide *subscription based* records databases in order for law enforcement, private investigators and other legal professionals to obtain records to aid them in their work. However, as valuable as the Internet is in investigative work, it is only one of many tools than an investigator uses. Usually, their most valuable tool is just plain old-fashioned footwork.

The investigator gathers information as the search progresses until the birthparent or adoptee is identified and located. The client is informed, and the next step, if desired, is contact.

Making Contact

In our opinion, contact is a very personal decision: *whether* to reach out and *how* to reach out. Occasionally, after going through an entire search, we have had our client decide not to have contact, maybe because they were simply curious and once their mystery is solved, it is enough just knowing—or perhaps they discovered something during the investigation that led them to change their mind about contact.

For the individual who decides to forge ahead with contact, *how* to make contact is a very personal choice that must be made thoughtfully. There are scads of books and articles written on the fine art of making initial contact. Some offer fantastic advice, and alternatively, we believe, some should just be burned! It is our opinion, an opinion that we've formed through years of experience acting as intermediaries, that contact, regardless of who makes it, should be approached discreetly, respectfully and considerately.

There are those who will say that it's one's *right* to barge right in and demand that the other person speak with them or meet with them. We believe that no one has the *right* to force himself or herself on another person. First of all, if it has been made clear that your search subject does not want contact, and if phone calls, letters or visits are made repeatedly, or identities are made public in newspapers or on the Internet, it can lead to charges of stalking and one can wind up in serious legal trouble. Secondly, and most importantly, what kind of healthy relationship can possibly be forged when a person is being pressured to do something against their will?

Now, that being said, we do believe that it *is* a person's *right* to *reach out* to another person and let them know that if they are interested in knowing you, that you are available for that. Or, if they could at least provide any medical history, you'd appreciate it. It's fine to let someone know you have been thinking of them and hope they've been thinking of you, too. It's just not okay to push for contact if it's been made clear that your search subject needs more time to decide, or flat out has no desire to meet you.

The only time we feel it is inappropriate to reach out to someone is when that someone is a minor child. If it's necessary to relay critical medical information, then indirectly notifying the adoptive parents through the original agency that handled the adoption, or a Confidential Intermediary, is perfectly acceptable and would probably be greatly appreciated. But searching for, identifying and contacting the young child could be very alarming to both the child and the parents. Contacting a minor child directly would be quite unethical, not to mention being illegal in some states.

We have worked with adoptive parents assisting their minor children who want contact with their birthparents, but again, we were working with adults. The bottom line is this: choice for contact must be by mutual consent between adults.

When contact is made, we feel that the key is to work through an intermediary who considers the emotions of all involved. When we first contact a birthmother, you can almost feel her on the phone line revert back to that terrified 16-year-old kid who relinquished her baby years ago. Adoptees may face other emotional challenges, such as an extreme fear of rejection or other buried emotions.

Just throwing triad members together without any preparation or guidance can be a recipe for disaster. They may say and do things that they would regret just minutes later. But that could be too late. In our work, we have had to do more than just find people. We have had to facilitate the contact between biological parents and adult children in a way that gives everyone involved the best possible opportunity to connect. The results, as you'll read in the true stories that follow, have been heartwarming, occasionally sad, and quite often surprising.

Beware Of The Woe-Sayers

It is only natural that once a person begins to entertain the idea of searching, that they will want to know more about the process and subsequent reunions. There are plenty of words of wisdom, available in the forms of books, articles and Internet websites, written by triad members that have already made contact. One thing we've noticed is that so many of these tales are negative portrayals of searches & reunions. Horror stories of reunions gone terribly wrong or painful rejections. This does make sense, because, really, those who have had wonderful or even just relatively quiet reunions don't have much to talk about once the search is over. They are no longer searching and have gone on about the business of living their lives, glad that the all-consuming, sometimes roller-coaster ride of a search is over and they have closure about their biological family. It is always a joy to find an article that was written by someone detailing his or her journey with a happy outcome. Sadly, though, those woeful stories are more prevalent because the writer needs to 'vent' as there was no peaceful resolution to their search. It may be the only way they can overcome the grief, or even anger, that they may be feeling. The author may even feel that others searching may need to be warned about a possible bitter outcome. Countless clients have expressed fears of going ahead with their own search after hearing some of these negative stories.

A public affairs pamphlet from 1969, titled '*You and Your Adopted Child*' states:

> Instances of extreme curiosity and concern almost never happen . . . however, should a youngster ever raise the question, it is important, of course, to make it very clear that a search is unrealistic and can lead to unhappiness and disillusionment.

Our advice is simple: Don't read those stories on the Internet—they can scare you to death. Also, don't give much thought to that well-meaning person who wants to warn you because they know someone whose life was ruined because of meeting their biological family. Your search is individual to you. No two searches are ever the same, no two outcomes are ever the same—they can't be, because no two people are ever the same. Can someone guarantee that your search will have the exact outcome you hope for? Of course not! But your journey in your search is *your* individual journey and no one else's experience should hinder you.

Closures

Most of our clients have had what they consider successful closures to their searches. Most of the people we've found were delighted to be found. Most of them were also scared, but went ahead with contact anyway and were glad they did, because they were able to let go of the burden of fear that had been weighing them down for so many years.

Some were *not* glad to be found and denied contact. Sadly, a few were found too late.

You will see from reading these stories that, even if a search subject denies contact or if a search results in finding the subject is deceased, there can still be a silver lining in that story.

CHAPTER 2

Ava's Own Story

The Other Sister

Little did Ava realize that her personal experience in 1990 with finding her biological sister would help propel her and her daughters into careers as private investigators specializing in adoption searches.

A Secret Revealed To Ava

After my father died in 1990, I discovered that I had a sister I never knew existed. My dad, Buster, was a hill man born in 1907 and raised in the beautiful Ozark Mountains of Arkansas, in the time when men fought to live by their own law—and he definitely was no exception.

Buster was a proud, confident and good-looking man of Scotch-Irish and American Indian descent. With a wry sense of humor, he had many friends and was known throughout the hills to be a 'man of his word.' His friends and neighbors could always count on him for any kind of help and he would have shared his last bite of food with even a stranger. Although he was not always, he could be very kind and compassionate, especially to children. I remember one cold, winter day when he went into the general store and bought a pair of long cotton stockings and gave them to me to give to a barelegged playmate whose parents were on hard times. (Harder times than we all had then in the 1930's were very hard indeed.)

That's one way to describe my dad.

On the other hand, he was a hard-drinking man who had as many enemies as he did friends. He had an explosive temper along with a mean streak, and was always looking for a fight. He was a gambler, ran whiskey and had a few shoot-outs with the sheriff before he was called upon to serve his country in the U.S. Navy during World War II. I loved him dearly, but was also scared to death of him. He didn't hesitate to pull off his belt and use it to discipline his children. It was not easy being his daughter.

A Picture From the Past

After Dad's death, I went to visit my uncle Ray, his youngest brother and the only one of his ten siblings that was still living. Uncle Ray showed me an old picture of Dad taken in the 1920's. He was sitting on the side of a sawmill, very young and handsome, sporting one of those old-fashioned newsboy type caps. He was holding the hands of a pretty young girl standing in front of him, wearing a white dress and plainly pregnant—and she was *not* my mother.

Uncle Ray told me that when my grandmother became old and near the end of her life, she gave him the picture and told him it was of Buster and the young girl who had gotten pregnant by him—and that the girl had later given birth to a daughter. Grandma had kept the picture all those years and she entrusted Uncle Ray to keep the secret. He kept the secret well, not even letting Buster know he had the picture. He felt it was now time we knew.

I knew I must find that baby girl, who would now be in her sixties, and I began to trace back in time. My first clue in finding my

sister was the sawmill in the picture; I remembered that one of Dad's cousins, Edith, who now lived in Missouri, had told me that when she was a little girl Dad had come down from the mountains one summer to stay with them and work in a sawmill with her father, his uncle. That was in 1924, nearly 70 years earlier.

I immediately called Edith on the phone and asked her, "Do you remember ever hearing that Dad got a girl pregnant when he was staying with your family that summer working at the sawmill?"

She was surprised, "Oh! I had forgotten all about that, but, yes, since you mention it, yes, I *do* remember, but I was so little, I didn't know who the girl was. However, I have a friend, Charlie, who still lives there—and he remembers *everything*. I'll call and ask him right now."

Arkansas People Remember Everything

After only a few minutes Edith called back and said she had talked to Charlie, who was well into his 90's and still sharp as a tack. He remembered clearly the time when Buster came to work at the sawmill. She recounted the conversation:

> *"Charlie, did you ever hear that Buster got a girl pregnant when he was staying with my family?"*
>
> "Yes, I remember that very well."
>
> *"Do you know who the girl was?"*
>
> "Yes, I know who she was."
>
> *"Who was she, Charlie?"*
>
> "She was my sister, Lily."

Edith was stunned at this news and asked "What happened, Charlie?"

> "Well, she was 15 and Buster was about 16 or 17 and he didn't want to get married, so he took out for the hills. When my Dad found out my sister was pregnant, he got his shotgun and went a-huntin' for Buster to kill him. We all liked Buster and didn't want Dad to shoot him, so we helped him hide out until he made his getaway back to the mountains. My sister married another man shortly before the baby, a little girl, was born."

Charlie said that before he could give her his niece's address, he would call Lily, who was now widowed and living in another state, and make sure it was alright with her if he gave Buster's family her daughter's phone number.

On the phone with Charlie, Lily was surprised at his question, but freely gave her consent, saying since it had all happened so many years ago, it didn't matter anymore. Charlie gave this message and phone number to Edith, who relayed it on to me.

The Other Sister

My other sister's name is Lola and she has lived in California since she was 17 years old, in the same area where Dad, my mother and the five of us children had lived during the same years. I wondered if I had passed her on the street, or maybe even talked to her without knowing who she was.

By the time I called Lola, her mother had already called her and she was expecting to hear from me. She told me that she had always known her biological father's name, and when I asked her why she didn't ever try to find him or any of his family, she responded:

> "Mother always told me that my father got killed in a car accident when she was pregnant with me. I didn't know he had any other family."
>
> She told me her mother and stepfather had somehow obtained a birth certificate for her with his name as her father, although he had never adopted her. She also told me that her early life was very unstable. She had several brothers and sisters, but her stepfather was a hard man who ruled the roost. She went to live with an aunt when she was only thirteen, later moving to California. I told her how bad I felt for her, growing up apart from us, but I also told her it had not been an easy life for us, either.

Still, I just could not understand how Dad could have known all those years that he had another daughter and didn't try to find her. In spite of his harsh ways, we all knew he loved us and doted on us most of the time. I felt sad that I didn't know Lola growing up.

My mother and dad were married in 1927, and their first child, a daughter, was born in 1928. When I found out about Lola, I called my older sister and she said that our mother had told her many years ago about Dad getting his young sweetheart pregnant. After our mother died, my sister had asked Dad about it but he seemed confused and said he wasn't sure that there ever was a baby. I often wonder who told Mother. I don't think Dad did, so maybe it was my Grandma, his mother.

Edith told me that Lola's mother and stepfather were good friends with her parents and they came often to visit. She said her parents adored Lola and now she knows why. Lola was actually their great niece. It must have been Edith's father, who was a brother to Grandpa, that gave Grandma the picture.

What's amazing is that the whole process of identifying, locating and making contact with my sister all happened in the space of one afternoon. We stayed in touch after that, calling each other often.

Finally a Face!

In March of 1992, for my 60th birthday, my family threw me a huge surprise party—and what a surprise it was! The morning of my birthday, my girls sent me to a spa for a makeover. My husband Bob came to pick me up that afternoon and I still had those pedicure things separating my toes, so I just wore them home. As we drove up to the house, I could see smoke billowing up over the rooftop from the backyard and I said, "Oh, my God, the house is on fire!" I jumped out of the car and as I hobbled barefoot through the house and on into the backyard, a live band started up and there were over a hundred of my friends and relatives gathered near a huge barbeque grill that was causing all the smoke.

I burst into tears when I first saw my two sisters, Jo and Mary, and sister-in-law, Chuckie, who all had traveled from their homes in California. The next person my eyes lit on was Lola, I knew her instantly, and the tears really flowed then. She looks so much like Dad, and I wish he could have known her. We also found out that we are a lot alike. We have a similar sense of humor and she cooks just like I do.

Lola's Side Of The Story

We have gotten especially close to Lola's daughter, Karen, and from her we found out how Lola was affected when I contacted her:

> "Lola was shocked that she had other family. She had made up stories such as her father was dragged to death by a plow, or he had died in an airplane crash. She was embarrassed about being illegitimate. When Aunt Ava contacted her, it was like a door opened. She never thought she was a very special person, and to have someone seek her out was overwhelming. It turns out they have similar personalities. Both were 'women libbers' before that was even a word."

After Lola moved to California, she married a good man who provided well for her. Together, they made a beautiful and happy home in which they raised his two daughters from a previous marriage and a daughter of their own, Karen. Now a widow, Lola is the center of her family and dearly loved by her daughters and her grandchildren.

It was important to me to find Lola and include her in the family from which she had been excluded all those years. I admit that my feelings for her are different from the ones that I have for the two sisters I grew up with, but, just the same, I feel a kinship with her and I love her.

I had no idea this reunion would help propel us into a career as private investigators, but that is exactly what it did. I'm sure it didn't hurt that this reunion happened so easily. If only all our cases could be so simple and straightforward.

Judy and Kristen—Our 'New' Aunt

Growing up, we were fortunate to be part of a large, close knit family; our aunts and uncles were more like our 'extra' parents, and our cousins were like sisters and brothers. Every Christmas, Thanksgiving, Birthday, Easter, etc. was celebrated together. Grandma was the glue that held us all together. Our family was saddened by her loss in 1983, and again seven years later when Grandpa passed away.

We were stunned when Mom told us she possibly had a sister she had never known about, and, of course, were both so excited! We had aunts and uncles that we loved dearly and had been close to all our lives, and getting a chance at having one more who might be like them would just be a cherry on top! We pleaded, "You *have* to find her, Mom—get on the phone!"

Mom, being from Arkansas, either knows, or knows of, just about everyone in the state. (We love research cases from Arkansas because Mom can make a few calls and solve the case in nothing flat!) We remember the day she started the search for her mystery sister so clearly, both of us sitting on Mom's bed watching and hanging on every word as she made the calls to various old-timers from Arkansas—then, just like that, she found her sister, Lola. She called her and we listened as they began to talk as if they had known each other always. They called each other often after that.

On Mom's 60th birthday in 1992, we planned a surprise party for her and since most of our relatives were coming from California for the event, we knew we just had to have Lola there, too. Although Mom and her sisters had all talked with Lola on the phone, none of our families had actually met. If we could pull it off, it would not only be a surprise for Mom, but a reunion for the whole family.

As aunts, uncles and cousins all arrived from California to cram into Kristen's tiny apartment the night before the party, Lola and her husband, Alan were there, too. The night was magical as we all laughed and cooked for the party the next day. As the excitement built, we all expressed little twinges of guilt that Mom was sitting, unsuspecting at home watching TV, and having no idea what was happening less than a mile from her! It would have only been made better if she were there with all of us. All Mom knew is that she had been trying to call her sisters in California all night and no one was home—we'd all freeze when the phone rang and contain our laughter as she'd tell Kristen, "I just can't imagine where everyone is—I am starting to get worried—and do you know where Judy is?" Finally our aunt Mary called her from Kristen's house, pretending to be at home in California. It was late when everyone left for their respective motels and I don't think any of us slept a wink all night, so happy and excited for the gift Mom was about to receive.

The next day was so perfect—Mom didn't have a clue as we sent her for a birthday makeover with promises of having a big birthday dinner with friends that night. When she returned home that afternoon, she found over a hundred of our family and friends in the backyard, and when the band started up with '*Happy Birthday,*' everyone cleared back from Lola, and as Mom's eyes lit upon her—she didn't even have to ask who she was. That was the soggiest rendition of Happy Birthday ever sung. Everyone was crying as Mom and Lola hugged and hugged.

We have all enjoyed a close relationship with Lola and her daughter, Karen (Alan has since passed away). Granted, Lola wasn't there to holler at or kiss us as children, and we don't share memories with Karen of hair-pulling fights or playing dolls together, but they are our family just the same and we are glad they came into our lives—better late than never!

CHAPTER 3

Lindsay's Search

A Personal Transformation

One morning in the summer of 1993, before we opened our private investigation agency, Ava was sitting at her desk in her bedroom working on the financial accounts for her husband's contracting company, when Lindsay unexpectedly came in the room, and without saying a word, put a stack of papers on the desk in front of Ava.

Lindsay was the girlfriend of Ava's grandson (and Judy's son), Keith. She was a pretty, petite girl with dark hair and very light freckled skin. Coming and going with the rest of the kids in Ava's lively household, Lindsay was like a part of their family. She had just celebrated her 21st birthday, was a student at Scottsdale Community College and worked part time at a fast food restaurant.

Although we treated Lindsay as part of our family, she was generally standoffish, and sometimes seemed downright cold—even to Keith. Although she always attended our big family get-togethers, she was usually reserved and seemed uncomfortable with everyone's frequent hugs and pats, almost flinching at being touched. We all just ignored her reactions and kept on hugging and patting, anyway. Keith and Lindsay had been friends since high school and Keith, who genuinely liked Lindsay, always excused her aloofness, saying that Lindsay 'didn't know who she really was.' At the time, no one realized how right he was.

The papers that Lindsay put on Ava's desk that morning were all of her adoption documents. Lindsay had prodded her mother for years for information about her birth family, but everything had always been very secretive, until just the day before when Lindsay's mother suddenly revealed to her where her adoption papers were hidden in her father's den. She also told her that she and Lindsay's father were going out of town for a week and Lindsay could do what she wanted with the papers, as long as she had them back in place by the time they got back home.

Lindsay knew that Ava, who clearly assumed the role of *Mom* with almost everyone, could be counted on for help. Over the years she had provided shelter to many juvenile runaways and helped them make peace with their parents, loaned them money in a pinch, took their collect phone calls, etc. and always had a few extras at the dinner table. It was no surprise to anyone that Lindsay turned to Ava when she needed help. Although Ava knew that Lindsay had very good parents who had provided her with a comfortable, upper middle-class upbringing, it was clear to everyone that knew Lindsay that she was somewhat troubled in her life. Maybe finding her birth family would set free the many emotions that Lindsay seemed to hold locked within herself.

Lucky Timing?

Lindsay's adoption papers indicated that Catholic Charities of Maryland had facilitated her adoption, so Ava made a call to them and, of course, was told that the adoption was sealed and no information could be given. However, they did have a mutual consent registry that allowed adult adoptees and birthparents to register--but information would be divulged only if both parties had signed up and consented to a reunion. Lindsay registered immediately, however if her parents had not already signed up giving their consent, the wait could be long and agonizing, as Lindsay soon found out. Lindsay returned her adoption papers to their hiding place and began the wait, without much hope.

Lindsay's search took place before Research Etc was founded and we were unable to find any information on her birthparents, unlike today when Research Etc can access dozens of private databases and other information sources to complete a search in usually a very short time.

A Call for Lindsay

Months later in the spring of 1994, the phone rang at Ava's house early one morning and her husband answered it. She heard him say they must have the wrong number as there was no Lindsay here, and upon hearing the name 'Lindsay,' Ava grabbed the phone from him before he could hang up. It was a nun calling from the Catholic Charities in Maryland who said that she had just connected Lindsay's name with her birthmother, and had already phoned the birthmother who was open to contact with Lindsay. However, she had to talk to Lindsay in person to verify she wanted contact, too. Ava took her phone number and excitedly called Lindsay, who drove over to Ava's house in record time. Lindsay nervously made the call and, after all the long months of waiting, and in less than a minute, she had her birthmother's name, Maggie, and her phone number. Lindsay wrote it all down and handed the information to Ava, saying calmly, "We'll call later." By this time Ava knew Lindsay well enough to know that, although her face showed no emotion, she was extremely excited and her heart was probably pounding a mile a minute. Lindsay had become more and more dear to Ava over the long months they had waited for this call.

From the phone call, Ava found out that Lindsay's reunion was delayed because at the very same time Lindsay contacted the Catholic Charities and registered her name, her birthparents were registering theirs. Both of their consent forms came in at the same time and checked against the existing consent registry for a possible match, without the Registrars making the connection. The two forms were then separately added to the registry, put back in the file, and not looked at again until months later.

Even though they had no physical contact for over twenty years, was there still some kind of connection between birthmother and child? Was Lindsay receiving some invisible signal, or possibly was she sending one that triggered her birthmother to act at the exact same time after so many years?
In our work over the years, we've found that this thought is not as unusual as it might sound. Whether you want to call it psychic or spiritual or simply biological, we've seen evidence of this kind of link or synchronization between birthparents and adoptees too often to dismiss it as coincidence.

That same night after they got the call from Catholic Charities, Lindsay came back and said, "Let's call Maggie." She couldn't make the call from her house, as she hadn't told her parents that she had found her birthmother, and she wouldn't have, anyway. Lindsay was too closed in on herself, too armored against the outside world, too shy to make the call herself, but she trusted Ava to do and say the right things while she listened, and for Ava to "just tell me what she sounds like."

Seeing that Lindsay was pretty much paralyzed with fear, Ava agreed and they made the call from her bedroom, a favorite place for the kids to gather while Ava worked at her desk. While Ava made the call, Lindsay got up on the bed and curled up against the headboard with her feet drawn up under her and her hands tucked under her chin. It was as if she was that tiny baby again at the time of her adoption.

Ava called Maggie and was instantly drawn to her warm voice. Ava explained that Lindsay was there in the room with her, but she was too emotional to talk. Maggie completely understood. Lindsay listened as they talked and a big smile began to form across her face.

A Thousand Questions

Maggie and Lindsay's birthfather, Rocky, were 'hippie' college student sweethearts in the 1970's. When she became pregnant, Rocky couldn't face the responsibility of marriage and fatherhood. Maggie understood his feelings, and although it was left up to her to cope the best she could, they remained friends. Maggie's family was a straight-laced Catholic family with a respected social standing in Baltimore. Her father was an attorney; her only sister was a nun. They were shocked and embarrassed when she told them she was pregnant and offered her no support in keeping the baby, but they would pay her expenses in the birth and adoption process. Although Maggie desperately wanted to keep her, she felt she had no other choice but to relinquish her baby, a little girl she named 'Mary.'

After the baby was born, Maggie and Rocky eventually drifted apart and lost touch. She moved to Colorado where she was employed by the state, working with children in foster care. Maggie married there and had three children, but she could not forget her first baby and the memory constantly tugged at her heart. She and her husband eventually divorced and she now lived alone with her children; Jake, 16, Carol, 14, and Mike, 12.

When twenty-one years had passed since the adoption, and 'Mary' became an adult, Maggie acted on the promise she had made to herself twenty-one years before. She located Rocky, who was now living in Connecticut, called him and simply said, "Rocky, let's go find our baby." Without hesitation, he replied, "Yes, let's do." They contacted the Catholic Services and signed the birth registry together. Although they had separated so many years before, Maggie and Rocky have always remained friends.

As Maggie and Ava concluded their phone conversation, Maggie asked her to tell Lindsay that she could call her collect any time, and she was open to as much contact as Lindsay wanted. Anything Lindsay wanted, she wanted, too. Maggie could not stop herself from calling Lindsay 'Mary.' That name had been in her heart too long to call her anything else.

The next night, Lindsay was back at the house with a long list of things she wanted to know from Maggie, but she wanted Ava to call and ask them. She just couldn't work up the courage to talk. So back to the bedroom they went and Ava called Maggie again. This happened for three or four nights and Lindsay had gotten comfortable with this process of sitting on the bed with her arms wrapped around herself, listening and smiling as Ava talked with Maggie on the phone.

However, on about the fifth night, when Ava made the call, Maggie wasn't home and her daughter Carol answered the phone. Like her mother, Carol had a sweet and warm voice, so Ava just held out the phone to Lindsay and said, "Here, Lindsay, your sister wants to talk to you." Ava knew from her conversations with Maggie that her children had always known about 'Mary' and they were eager to know their older sibling. Lindsay was so taken by surprise, she took the phone and the two sisters began to talk excitedly and freely. They talked about hair color and freckles and other similar traits and Lindsay found that she was never a 'deep, dark secret,' but instead had always been very much a part of their lives.

The next night, from Ava's bedroom, Lindsay finally spoke with the woman who had given birth to her. What Ava remembers most from that first conversation between birthmother and daughter is that it was the first time she had ever seen Lindsay giggle. Already a much-needed change was beginning to take place.

Twenty-One Letters Never Sent

Just a few days later, Maggie and her three children drove to Scottsdale to meet Lindsay. Lindsay had told her parents by this time, but they were not ready to meet her birthmother, so Lindsay made plans to meet Maggie at Ava's home. After checking into a hotel, Maggie and the children got to Ava's about 4 p.m.

Maggie is a very pretty woman with dark hair and fair skin just like Lindsay. Judy and Kristen were also there and they all introduced themselves and hugged and settled down to wait for Lindsay. And they waited. Soft drinks and snacks were served and, still, they waited. After a couple of hours, the talk pretty much ran out as everyone's excitement turned to apprehension, but still no Lindsay. Maggie was very understanding. It seems they were probably very much alike.

It was about 6: 30 p.m. before they heard a car pull up in the driveway. Ava went out to meet Lindsay and saw she had a girlfriend along, apparently for support. Taking Lindsay by the arm, both furious and relieved, she whispered, "Get in the house!" Lindsay entered the house first to see Kristen, Judy, Keith, Amy, Shawn, Maggie, Jake, Carol and Mike all crowded in the entry hall to greet her. Lindsay sort of let out a little gasp, turned around and threw her arms around Ava! On one hand, everyone thought this was a strange reaction from Lindsay, but on the other, it was the first time they had seen her voluntarily hug *anyone*, so that was already something.

Ava hugged her tight for just a minute before she turned her around and said, "Lindsay, this is Maggie." They smiled at each other and the children introduced themselves. Lindsay remained tense at first. Again, it was the kids, her birth siblings, who helped her relax. Judy ordered pizza and all the kids went out on the patio and soon much talking and laughing was heard. The next afternoon, Maggie and Lindsay spent time together, just the two of them. Maggie gave Lindsay a bundle of letters, 21 in fact, that she had written to her on every birthday. She, of course, could never mail them, but had saved them in hopes this very day would come.

The Real Lindsay Revealed

After that meeting, Lindsay seemed to make a 180-degree turn in her life. She became very warm and communicative. It was an instantaneous change, apparent to everyone but Lindsay herself, who has never seemed to realize what a different person she has become since that meeting. It was as if she pulled off a mask she'd been wearing all these years, to reveal her true self. She would hug us first when she saw us, and she would smile, smile, and smile. Up until she got married, and long after she and Keith stopped dating, she would drop in at our family parties, especially at Christmas, bringing her current boyfriend, and she was just a part of our family. She still is.

There's no doubt that Lindsay's positive transformation was the result of meeting Maggie, as Maggie is that way herself—friendly, warm and compassionate. According to Lindsay, her mother and father were more reserved. We felt that since Lindsay had always wanted to please them, she had patterned herself after them, even though a reserved personality was unnatural for her. But after meeting Maggie, she either realized or remembered who she was and became much more natural and open with her feelings.

On another level, we know that Maggie had held Lindsay and talked to her as a newborn. We wondered, were they physically bonded at that time and had Lindsay been missing this connection in her life?

When Maggie relinquished her baby, she didn't know that she had other choices, as adoption was the only option given to her. She knows that today there are many choices open to unwed mothers, and they can take a much larger role in the decisions to be made.

A few months after Maggie's visit, Rocky flew in from Connecticut to Colorado and he and Maggie and the children all drove to Arizona to see Lindsay. We had them over for dinner, and enjoyed sharing their happiness. Rocky is divorced and has two more daughters. He is a very nice looking, intelligent and likeable man, and he and Lindsay soon made friends. She later went to Connecticut for a visit and to meet her two young sisters. The girls have also been out to Arizona to visit with Lindsay and stayed with her and her parents, who welcomed them with open arms, although they are still not ready to meet Lindsay's birthparents. After being the baby in her family, Lindsay suddenly became "big sister" to five siblings, a role she relishes, and she keeps in close touch with all five of them.

This is an excerpt from a letter Ava later received from Rocky a year later:

> *Dear Ava,*
>
> *One year ago today you called me (with Lindsay at your side) for the first time. I could not let this anniversary pass without thanking you again for all you did for Lindsay, Maggie, and me...hope your Mother's Day was special. You have a lot of "kids" that are better for having known you...Love to you and yours, Rocky*

Maggie also sent us a card around the same time, she wrote:

> *Dear Ava, Judy and Kristen,*
>
> *Nothing could compare with what you gave me last year—the gift of a lifetime! I thank you all so much! Helping Lindsay find me—you found my missing part—a piece of my heart. And you let us into your lives so warmly—Thank you—forever!... Lots and lots of love,*
>
> *Maggie*

Keith and Lindsay started dating others while they were in college, but managed to keep their deep friendship. Years later, Lindsay married one of Keith's best friends and they are all like a part of our family. Maggie and the children came to Lindsay's wedding, and although her children Jake, Carol and Mike went to the reception afterward, Maggie chose not to attend. She felt it was Lindsay's parents' day and she didn't want to intrude. Maggie has also remarried and Lindsay, her husband and children attended the wedding in Colorado. Lindsay says that Maggie seems more like a favorite aunt than a mother and she finds her easy to talk to. They remain very close. Lindsay is a mature, loving wife and gentle mother. She and her parents have a close relationship and they dote on their grandchildren.

We believe Lindsay finally *knows who she really is!*

CHAPTER 4

JD's Search

Cracking the Code

One of our most challenging search cases came in the form of JD, a husky good-looking guy in his early 30's. JD had sandy blond hair and a friendly engaging way about him. Like many adoptees, he had good, loving parents and a comfortable life. After all, most adoptees are extremely desired by their adoptive parents.

Medical History Needed

JD was married and his wife was pregnant and they wanted to be able to fill out their medical history for the pediatrician. This was his only motivation for searching for his birthmother. Nothing more dramatic than that.

JD had his Non-Identifying Information (NIDI) that is often made available to adoptees through the courts or the adoption agency. The purpose of NIDI is to give the adoptee some sense of who their birth family is, without revealing their identity. But NIDI can still be helpful in tracking down the birth family, as it provides background information that can serve as clues. This may include circumstances of the adoption, medical background, social history and occupations.

The trouble is that NIDI is notoriously unreliable. Mothers may falsify facts in order to make the adoptee sound more socially acceptable to potential families, as well as to make their own circumstances more sympathetic. You might be surprised to know how many birthmothers were noted to be a '*good Christian girl taken advantage of during an inebriated state . . .*'

In one case, a birthmother had falsified her name at the adoption agency. This was because she had already relinquished a baby for adoption at this agency once before, and she was embarrassed to be in the same situation again. Without realizing it, she correctly listed her other children's real names and dates of birth, giving her identity away.

Sometimes Non-Identifying Information is incorrectly recorded due to carelessness. We once got information showing a birthmother was from California. We tracked hundreds of women who were potential matches in California, before evidence turned up showing she was actually from Kansas. It is safe to say, from our experience, NIDI can provide invaluable clues or it can lead you on a wild goose chase.

In another instance, the NIDI from an adoption agency in New York had reversed the mother and father's information. We knew the father wasn't a *housewife* as the form indicated, but had the person who'd recorded this only reversed that category? Or the entire form?

Too Many Blanks

In JD's case, the Non-Identifying Information was extremely limited. Written by typewriter in 1967, all the names of people and places had been cut out with an Exacto knife, leaving blanks in the paper. Someone went to great lengths to be secretive.

JD's adoption papers, given to him by his parents, showed that he was born in Alabama. Beyond that, all we had to work with was this chopped up NIDI. Although we didn't voice our fears to JD, we thought "How in the world are we ever going to find this young man's birthmother?"

We quickly realized we had a huge puzzle on our hands. When we blew up a copy of the NIDI by 400%, we found one factor working in our favor: by cutting out the information instead of blacking it out with ink, some vital clues had been left behind. The parts of the letters that rose above or dipped below the line of type were still on the page.

The small letters that rose above had to be one of these: *b, d, f, h, k, l* or *t*. Since the top of a dot could also show up, we included *i and j*.

On the other hand, small letters that left remnants below the cutout had to be from among: *g, j, p, q*, or *y*.

Cracking the Code

We quickly determined that the mother's first name had eight letters, and the fourth letter was a *g, j, p, q*, or *y*. But the best clue was that her maiden name was six letters long—and had double letters in the middle that dipped below the lines—this had to be '*gg*.'

Then we decided to try to identify the birthmother's place of residence that was blanked out on JD's birth certificate. The first thing we did was to determine the number of letters in the town name by measuring off the number of spaces for letters. We found that the town had ten letters. We did the same with the county and found it had 12 letters.

We pulled out a map of Alabama and started playing mix and match. We searched for all the county names that fit the number of letters, and then identified the ones that fit the kind of letters, based on the tails and tips that had been left behind.

Once we had determined all the counties that would fit in the blank, we looked for all the towns in each of these counties that would fit the number and type of letters for that blank. There were literally hundreds of potential combinations, so we had no choice but to start working through them. It was extremely tedious work, but the more we got into it, the more stubborn and determined we were to discover just where JD's birthmother came from.

We worked on this all day and usually late into the night for several days. It was a challenge we couldn't let go of. Finally, after about 40 hours of this close forensics work, we felt confident that we had identified the town and county. The next step was to get confirmation.

Confirming a Hunch

The location we had zeroed in on was a very small town with only one high school in it. The NIDI had mentioned the birthmother's age, so we were able to determine the year she'd probably graduated from high school. It was time for Kristen to exercise her gift of gab talent.

She called the high school and a polite southern gentleman answered. She told him she was working on a reunion list for that class and asked if he could give her the names of every student registered in that class that year. He was very helpful and looked up the records. Thankfully he had the time on his hands to do it.

As the man read off the names, Kristen repeated them so that Judy and Ava could hear and test them against the number of spaces and the type of letters on the form. They went through about 25 names before the right one came along. When they found the one that fit, the first name had eight letters with the fourth letter dipping down, and the last name having '*gg*' in the middle, Judy and Ava were jumping up and down whispering, "Yes! Yes!"

To keep up appearances, Kristen had to listen to another 30 names before she was able to thank the nice man for his help and get off the phone.

We found the name, but now we needed corroboration. We ran the name in our national database and found that the date of birth was a match for the birthmother's age. The age of her younger sister, also provided in the Non-Identifying Information, matched up as well. From the Social Security Death Index, we identified potential grandparents for the birthmother. We looked up obituaries and saw the grandfather's profession was the same profession mentioned in the NIDI. He had a long obituary because he was a member of the town's city council and it gave plenty of details about the family. We now knew JD's birthmother's parents' first names as well, and they also fit into the spaces provided on the NIDI.

We knew we had found JD's birthmother. The next step was to call her. We could have found her number in our database, but as it turned out, she was listed in information. We updated JD on what we had found out and asked him how he wanted us to proceed, and he gave us the following instruction:

> "Tell her I don't want anything from her, just my medical history. Tell her I'm open to knowing her if she wants, but I understand if she doesn't."

He wanted to thank her for putting him in the home she did. He wanted her to know he was grateful for how he had been raised.

First Contact

Ava has a southern accent that people from that region respond to, so she was chosen to make the phone call to JD's biological mother. The first contact with a birthmother can be an extremely delicate matter, so every little thing helps. In the case of JD's birthmother, it wasn't going to be easy in any case.

Ava made the call that evening and JD's birthmother answered the phone. Ava identified herself and said, "I'm trying to locate a lady whose maiden name is Marjorie Dugger." When she said, "Yes, that is my name," Ava told her the purpose of her call,

Marjorie gasped, burst into tears, could barely speak, and became hysterical as she frantically asked:

> "How did you find out? Did you call my neighbors, my church, who? What do you want from me? Who else have you told about this?"

Ava tried to calm her and reassure her that she had talked to no one in Marjorie's home town, or, in fact, to anyone but her. She tried to explain that she was a professional investigator who represented Marjorie's birthson, and the utmost discretion had been used to protect both her and her birthson's privacy.

But Marjorie was distraught and in tears. She seemed convinced that Ava was trying to blackmail her. To her, this was such a deep, dark secret, our only possible motivation to search for her must have been for revenge or punishment of some kind.

Tearfully, she told Ava that it was graduation night for her daughter and she was just leaving for the ceremony and had a big party planned for afterwards. Ava felt terrible that this momentous event happened to be on the same night she made the call and she apologized profusely for intruding on such an important night for their family.

Ava emphasized to Marjorie that no one, least of all her birthson, wanted to intrude on her life and she asked her to please write down her phone number and call her the next day so they could straighten everything out.

However, later that night, Marjorie's husband called. He was beside himself with rage:

> "Whatever it is you want, you don't want to mess with me, girl! I can play hardball, if that's what you want. I'm a minister, but I can be tough! If I find out that you've spread this around town, you are going to be in plenty of trouble!"

Ava started talking over his rage in a calm voice, explaining that she was with a licensed private investigation agency, we were very discreet and confidential, etc., and she kept on talking to him until he had to be quiet to hear her say,

> "No one but your wife, her birthson, and you, know that we have contacted her. And you only know it because your wife told you. Otherwise you would never have known it from us. All of the information that we have compiled about your wife has been from public records. We have searched for her because the boy is going to be a father himself and needs his birthmother's medical records. He is not looking for a mother, nor does he wish to intrude on your lives or cause you any upset."

Anger drained away from the minister, no doubt a good man who was only trying to protect his family, as he listened intently to Ava. Then he asked her "Did you tell my wife this?" He then turned aside to his wife and said,

> "Honey, this boy only wants a family medical history from you."

But Marjorie still believed that a neighbor or a friend had somehow found out about the adoption and was trying to blackmail her. It was such a secret to her, such a shameful thing; she probably would have gone to any lengths just to keep it quiet.

"I don't want any contact," she said, and refused to give out any medical information.

In many cases, birthmothers say *no* initially when they are first contacted. About half the time, or more, they reconsider once they've thought it through. So Ava reminded Marjorie that she had our phone number and encouraged her to make contact with us at any time, now, or in the future.

Fears and Tears

Early, the very next morning, Marjorie called. She was in tears. Judy took her call and listened as Marjorie told her of how embarrassed she was at having a child out of wedlock and especially since her husband was the minister of their church. However, she still wanted to know about JD.

> "Does he have an education? Does he go to church? What does he look like? Is he in good health?"

In fact, after answering several of Marjorie's questions about JD's health, Judy realized that another fear might have occurred to Marjorie, such as maybe her birthson wanted a bone marrow transplant from her, or maybe some other difficult medical assistance. Again, Marjorie was terrified that this would expose her secret in her hometown.

Judy explained again that JD's wife was pregnant and reassured her that he only wanted to know the medical background, and that he didn't want to intrude on her life. But this wasn't enough to convince Marjorie, who promptly hung up on Judy.

It looked like this case was going nowhere. JD's birthmother simply had too much shame and fear. But then something we didn't anticipate happened—JD's birth *grandmother* got involved. She and her daughter Marjorie were the only two who knew about the pregnancy and adoption at that time. The birth grandmother had even handled all the arrangements for Marjorie's stay at the maternity home and the subsequent relinquishment and adoption placement.

After our call, a distraught Marjorie had called her mother for support, but when she heard the news, Marjorie's mother decided she wanted to *know* her grandson. She ordered her daughter to call us right back and tell us they wanted to discuss this some more. She expressed such an urgency, it was almost as if she feared the deal might expire or something.

Marjorie called again that same afternoon and, tearfully, told Judy she wanted to speak to JD. She was worried that he might have been offended by how she'd acted. She pleaded,

> "*Please* don't tell him I talked that way when you first called."

This is an example of the importance of having an intermediary to make first contact. Many things may be said at first that could be extremely hurtful. These words are often the result of the initial panic and confusion people experience when they are contacted unexpectedly. For many, it's like hearing from a ghost. A good intermediary is vital in breaking news and smoothing the way toward a successful reunion.

Not to say Marjorie still didn't have her issues. She didn't want JD to call her at home. She had three teenage daughters to whom she had long preached chastity and abstinence until marriage. She was terrified they'd find out she had failed to live up to her own high standards. So she said she would call back at the agreed upon time.

That was on a Saturday and we arranged for her to call our office the next afternoon and we would have JD there to take her call.

Birthmother and Son Speak

Very early on Sunday morning, the phone rang, waking Judy. It was an extremely nervous Marjorie calling before she went to church, she just had to know

> "Is he mad at me? Does he want to get back at me for what I've done?"

Her fears were not so unusual. We do a lot of handholding and comforting. Judy reassured her that JD felt no such inclinations, so Marjorie dried her tears, hung up and went to church. She called two more times after church, hours before JD was due to be at our office. Judy let her talk and kept reassuring and encouraging her. Marjorie was a complete wreck and Judy was worn out.

JD and his wife arrived at the office and, for the first time, our usually composed client was very nervous. When the phone rang, we answered and it was Marjorie. We gave the phone to JD and all went into an adjoining room so he could have some privacy. We could hear them talking, but couldn't make out actual words. By his composed tone, it sounded like he was trying to calm her down.

All of a sudden we plainly heard him say,

"You're going to have to lighten up, woman."

We all just fell over laughing. We had wanted so much to say that to her at some point along the way, but JD was the only one who was able to—and get away with it.

Afterward JD told us Marjorie had asked if he had a moustache, if he smoked and if he was a Christian, roughly in that order.

They spoke on the phone fairly often after that initial phone call, but now they no longer needed an intermediary.

Meeting in Palm Springs

Two months after their first conversation, JD flew to Palm Springs where he met Marjorie, her husband and three daughters who were vacationing there. The reunion went very well. Marjorie was so proud of JD and her husband was kind enough to welcome JD into his family. He called JD his son, which touched JD deeply.

Before leaving home on this trip, Marjorie had finally told her daughters about the son she had placed for adoption so long ago. Not surprisingly, for everyone except Marjorie, her girls were hardly scandalized by the news and were thrilled to have a big brother, which they'd always wanted. After they met him in Palm Springs, the girls called JD often and started coming to Arizona frequently to visit with him and his wife and new baby—their nephew. JD also made a trip to Alabama and got to meet his birth grandmother, who was delighted.

During our investigation, we discovered that Marjorie had embellished her story to her agency caseworker to make it appear that she had known and dated the birthfather for a long time, ultimately leaving him heartbroken. The truth was he was already engaged to another woman while Marjorie was pregnant.

The real picture that emerged from our research is of a very young woman who had entrusted herself to a man who had little caring for her, and of her desperation to cover up her error in any way possible. She had told her husband about the birth before their marriage, but she would never reveal the biological father's identity to anyone. Even though we had discovered his identity in our search, we did not reveal this knowledge to Marjorie, and JD was not the least bit interested in knowing him. He said that he was totally satisfied with the way his search had gone and was going no further.

The good news for Marjorie was that times have changed for the better. Her daughters didn't view their mother's pregnancy out of wedlock with the same stigma that Marjorie and her family at that time no doubt did. It was those shameful conditions that drove her into hiding a secret she might have concealed forever, had JD's wife not gotten pregnant and prompted him to learn his medical history. We believe that now Marjorie is able to see that shame as the paper tiger it really was.

CHAPTER 5

Cara's Search

A Sense of Self

A Troubled Beginning

Cara came into this world legally blind, on a cold, winter day in 1979 at a hospital in Providence, Rhode Island. At the age of two months, she was removed from her mother's custody and placed in foster care.

At the time of her removal, Cara's unnamed birthmother was in the company of a man who may or may not have been Cara's birthfather. Russell was a truck driver and Cara's mother had taken her newborn and gone on the road with him.

A couple of days into their trip, Russell realized that the baby could not see and it was he who insisted they stop and have a doctor examine her. The mother relented and somewhere along the road in Ohio they found a doctor's office. The doctor discovered severe cataracts and suspected the baby might have other disabilities. He contacted the Marietta, Ohio Children's Services, who suspected the baby had been neglected and they offered to take her into temporary foster care. It would later be told that Cara's mother had no intention of leaving her baby permanently; she simply felt that they could fix Cara's eyes and would give her back once she could see properly. Ultimately, her mother was found to be unfit to care for Cara, so the baby remained in foster care for the next six months.

A New Home

Following the six-month stay with Children's Services and a complete termination of her mother's parental rights, a couple who lived in the area adopted Cara. Linda and Ernie Collins had been on the waiting list for a very long time and were willing to accept a child with disabilities.

Cara's adoptive parents provided her with material stability and a comfortable home to grow up in, but over time it became clear that they harbored unrealistic expectations of her. Linda and Ernie treated her like a possession and whenever she would stray from their idea of the proper way a young child should behave, they would blame it on the fact that she was adopted, rather than the fact that she was simply a young girl being herself.

Cara's parents often reminded her, in a negative way, that she was adopted. When she asked about her birth family, they would tell her they didn't know anything about them, but would insinuate that she had come from less-than-desirable stock, which would understandably upset Cara.

With this kind of parenting, Cara was never really able to settle down and feel as if she belonged. Ironically, her parents' mean-spiritedness in regard to her birth family only fueled her desire to know the truth of why she had been placed for adoption. From the age of sixteen on, she was looking for ways to search for her birth family.

Cara's boundless energy helped her to overcome the negativity of her less than supportive family as well as her disability of limited vision. She became a studiously successful girl, and after graduating high school, she was accepted into college in Northern Ohio.

Disapproving Parents

Like a lot of teenage girls in the history of the world, Cara, at the age of 19, became pregnant out of wedlock while she was away at college. Once again, she was a disappointment to her parents. So much so that when she told Linda about her predicament, she and Ernie disowned Cara, and stated,

> "We really can't be surprised since you're adopted."

Cara told us that this was one of the most devastating periods in her life. At this most crucial of moments, when Cara really needed them, her mother and father totally rejected her, and removed themselves from her life. Strangely, Linda also chose this time to reveal to Cara her birth name: Maria Douglas.

Cara or Maria?

Cara has proven herself to be an amazing example of the human spirit prevailing over all opposition. She continued her education, at the same time raising her child on her own. And despite the heartache of her adoptive parents' rejection, she kept right on moving to know her own birth story.

Armed with her birth name, she wrote to the hospital where she was born and requested her records. She signed the letter with her birth name, 'Maria Douglas'—knowing they would never send Maria's personal information to a 'Cara Collins.'

She was required to submit a money order to pay for the photocopies, but when she went to the bank and got the money order, she forgot and signed with her own name instead of her birth name. The moment she dropped the envelope in the mailbox slot, she realized the mistake she had made and waited by the box for hours until the mailman came to pick up the mail. She begged and pleaded with him to return the envelope containing the money order to her so she could change the name, until he finally relented and handed it over to her. She made the corrections and put it back in the box.

Several weeks later, Cara received her birth records from the hospital. Though most of the records were jumbled up, they did list her birthmother's name, Cherry Douglas, along with an address and phone number. Then a few days later, she received her Non-Identifying Information from the adoption agency. Those records stated that her father was a 'young, thin, tall, brown-haired man on drugs.' Her mother was described as a 'thin, young, blond woman about 5'-5" tall.' Cara was named 'Baby Douglas.' It was in those records that Cara learned how she was taken from her mother and placed into foster care. She was beginning to collect pieces of her 'life-puzzle' and it inspired her to keep going.

Cara had traced the information she'd obtained from her birth records to Providence, Rhode Island. Soon after her marriage to Mike, a caring man who completely supported her drive to find her birth family, Cara and her new husband traveled to Providence for their honeymoon and to search for information about her birth family.

They visited the hospital where she was born and viewed the apartment her mother once lived in. But they were unable to find any more information on her birth family than Cara already had. Mike even placed an advertisement in the local newspaper, but they got no response. As honeymoon's go, it was an extremely frustrating trip. But now at least Cara was no longer alone in her search, and had her husband's love and devotion backing her.

Private Investigators Hired

Cara and Mike set aside money for a more thorough search for her birth family, despite it meaning they would have to live 'hand to mouth' at times. Shortly after their trip to Providence, they hired the services of an investigator in Ohio. He kept them on edge for months, and in the end never found anything that could help them identify her birth family. At one point, he attempted to extort extra money from them by pretending he had found some relatives, but Cara and Mike would have to come up with more money before he would reveal their identities. This tactic didn't set well with Cara, and following her gut instincts, she stopped working with that investigator, then and there.

Despite her many failed attempts, Cara knew that she had to keep going. She and Mike both now felt there was no more they could do on their own. They were living in Kentucky in 2003 where Cara was in college studying Communications and Human Services when she discovered our website on the Internet. She called us and we spoke at length, and found her to be an intelligent and very sweet woman with a wonderful sense of humor who had overcome enormous hurdles in her life. We agreed to help her with her search.

The Elusive Cherry Douglas

With the unusual advantage of already having a name and an address from the hospital records, we began the search for Cherry Douglas on the 18th of July 2003. Usually, the toughest part of any search is getting the name of the birth parent or adoptee, and it was a process that sometimes took many months. However, we thought, since we had already had the identifying information, finding this birthmother would be a snap. A 'snap' it was not.

Every clue we found in tracing our target led us down a dead end. We were, however, able to sketch a general portrait of who Cherry Douglas was and what her life had been like. We found addresses for her in Florida, Colorado, Oregon, North Carolina, Idaho and Nevada. She was a lifelong transient whose records showed that she had a total of three marriages and six children, whom she'd left scattered around the country with their respective fathers or in foster care. We found criminal records for her in two states.

The last known address we'd identified for her was in Boise,

Idaho. We located and talked to several people who knew her, and they all described her as a very troubled person who drank heavily and frequently worked as a prostitute. They also agreed that she had trouble choosing men who could really give her the love and stability she craved.

Meet The Family

We discovered an obituary for one of Cherry Douglas' ex-husbands who had lived in Colorado and it listed all of her children, who were also Cara's birth siblings—two brothers and three sisters. From just this one source, we were able to locate them all. The bad news was that none of them had seen or heard from their mother for at least three years.

Cara experienced quite a shock meeting and talking with her brothers and sisters, though we had to hand it to her, she kept her sense of humor all the way along. Not one of her siblings was mentally healthy or stable. They were all—as she described them—'street people,' and nothing like her. This is how she explained it in one of her letters to us:

> "I had never encountered people who lived like they did. I've been poor, but never so unstable. It would bother me not to know where my next meal was coming from, but it didn't seem to bother them in the least. Their kids go in and out of foster care routinely, and to my siblings, it's just their way of life."

Through meeting her brothers and sisters, she came to the realization that though her adoptive parents hadn't given her their love, they did give her a material stability she would always be grateful for.

Return to Sender

Cara managed to become close to one of her half-sisters, Laura. In one of their early conversations, Laura asked Cara what her favorite color was and when Cara said, 'purple,' Laura's eyes widened as she exclaimed that their mother loved purple and had always worn purple clothes when Laura was in her care.

Laura shared photos, trinkets that had belonged to Cherry, and also records of their mother's mental health issues. Cara learned that Cherry Douglas was not always competent. She suffered from bipolar disorder, as well as post-traumatic stress caused by a series of abusive men. She had been sexually molested as a young girl. The records also showed that though she drank alcohol throughout all her pregnancies, she apparently hadn't been as heavy of a drinker during her pregnancy with Cara as she had been later on with her other children.

Laura told Cara that she had sent her mother an invitation to her wedding, which had occurred the year before, but it was returned marked 'Return to Sender.' Laura admitted that the returned letter hadn't surprised her too much because her mother had a history of moving and having no contact for long periods, but she was sad that her mother had missed her wedding.

Cara, on the other hand, was concerned that their mother's whereabouts remained a mystery. Together, they decided to report her missing to the local police. They also put up missing person flyers all over the area she was last living in, to no avail.

The Search Continues

In early 2005, we located Cherry Douglas' most recent husband, Gary, who now lived in Little Rock, Arkansas. When we spoke with Gary by phone and explained that we were interested in the whereabouts of Cherry Douglas, he promptly hung up on us. Several more attempts yielded the same bizarre result. At that point, we gave his number to Cara and suggested she call him and try to talk with him. Gary had no problem speaking to Cara once she identified herself as Cherry's daughter and freely told her that Cherry didn't come home one day, so he just packed up and moved out without telling her, never seeing or hearing from her again. We wondered how alone and insignificant Cherry must have felt when the man she was married to could treat her disappearance so lightly.

We were still unable to locate Cherry, although she seemed to be all around and just one step ahead of us with every person we talked to. Our search led us to a woman who was using Cherry's Social Security number currently. We located her phone number, and Cara called her, explaining that she was trying to find Cherry. The woman coldly responded, "I'd stop looking for Cherry if I were you." *How chilling those words would become two years later.*

We tracked down information on Cherry's father, Daniel Douglas, and that led us to an obituary following his death in the 1970's, which named the funeral home that had conducted his final services. We called the home to see if they had a current listing of relatives for the Douglas family, especially Daniel Douglas' brother, Ronald. Although, the funeral director was puzzled, he gave us a last known address dating back to the 1970's.

We were able to trace the old address, but no new information turned up there, so a few days later, we called the funeral home again to see if they might have further information on the family. This second call from us apparently aroused the suspicions of the funeral director and he heatedly questioned our motives. As it turned out, the day after our first call, Ronald Douglas had died and his body was now there in the funeral home and they were in the process of planning his services.

Kristen was mortified! She got the impression they suspected we'd known him all along and had been waiting for him to die, that maybe we were after his estate.

We later learned that all of Cherry's children were named as Ronald Douglas' sole legal heirs and this matter is still at issue in the Rhode Island Court. Because Cara was adopted, the court has not yet decided whether she can legally inherit. Cara says that the money doesn't mean anything to her; what really matters and touches her heart is the fact that her siblings are fighting the court to split the estate equally among all of Cherry's children, regardless of the fact that one was adopted.

A Predictable Tragedy

On the 29th of June 2005, the Boise media reported that a decomposing body had been discovered wrapped in a comforter and stuffed in a plastic container in the backyard of a house. The man who lived in the house had just recently moved there and found the container among a pile of junk. When he opened the box and discovered its contents, he called the police. Initially, the police reported that the body was so badly decomposed they couldn't tell whether it was male or female. During the autopsy, a bracelet and a ring were discovered on the body, and authorities suspected that the body could be that of a woman.

A neighbor told reporters she had a hunch the box belonged to a man who had lived in the house some years ago. He was currently in prison, convicted for forging checks. Cara's sister, Laura, and her other siblings had already begun to suspect that the body might very well be that of their mother. Detectives had contacted Laura to tell her that a graduation ring engraved with the name 'Laura Andrew' had been found on the body. They'd traced it to her through her former high school. Laura told the police she had given her ring to her mother years ago, and knew that she always wore it. Laura was quoted in the newspaper as saying that the authorities had taken

DNA samples from the decomposing body and, she added, "They wouldn't have gotten a hold of me if it wasn't her."

The body was finally positively identified as that of Cherry Douglas. Cause of death was attributed to a seven-inch skull fracture. We couldn't help but feel the dreadfulness of how her life had been taken, the violence causing such a fracture, and the conflict that must have led to it—and the disturbed person who had inflicted the injury on her.

Cara was heartbroken by this horrifying news. For all her years of searching, all of her hopes, to end with a discovery like this—it was inconceivable.

Because our search for Cherry began around the same time that authorities determined she had been murdered, we contacted the investigating police detective. She requested that we turn over our complete file, along with names, addresses and phone numbers of all the people we had interviewed regarding Cherry and her whereabouts, and also our notes about what they had said at the time. Although authorities eventually interrogated the person they suspected of being responsible for her death, they reported there was not enough evidence to prosecute. Cherry's children wondered if the police were unwilling to pursue the case because Cherry Douglas, an addict and a prostitute, was considered a lost cause anyway, and her death was not a priority—not worth their time. Sadly, Cherry's children may never have closure by seeing their mother's murderer brought to justice.

A Sense of Self

Though the outcome of Cara's search for her birthmother turned out to be a shocking disappointment for her, she told us that she did obtain a sense of closure. She went through intense grief after her birthmother's body was identified, but she felt that, at the very least, she had come to know who her birthmother had been. Obtaining the facts about her origins has helped Cara accept herself in an essential way and has improved her self-esteem tremendously. She had always wanted to know the truth and now she knew it all.

Cara recently achieved her Master's Degree in Communication Research Studies. She and Mike now have four children, three of whom they adopted; Jacob, George, Piper and Kelsey, and she describes them as "my world and my light."

In a recent letter that we received from Cara, she wrote;

> "I have a better outlook about why I'm here and I am able to put the pieces of my life into perspective. The truth is always better than the unknown. . . . While I agree that my story is sad and often gut-wrenching, I am forever grateful to you for all your help. Without you, I would never have known. Even as bad as the pain is, it is better than being in the dark."

CHAPTER 6

Fred's Search

Flesh of My Flesh

Fred's story is special to us because he was the first *birthfather* that we helped to find a daughter that was placed for adoption. We particularly love this case because it shows that a guy, who described himself as once being immature and irresponsible, can grow and become the caring, considerate man who contacted us, seeking to reconnect with his birthdaughter.

A Birthfather Seeks to Reconnect

Fred first called us in 1995. At that time, he was living in a small town in Connecticut with his long time love, Rita. Rita owned an art gallery and Fred helped her run it. When he traveled to Arizona on business, the last thing on his mind was trying to find his birthdaughter while he was here. But sometimes the thing you least expect can fall right in your lap.

Arizona was where he and his former wife were living when they had relinquished their daughter; so visiting Phoenix brought all the memories back to him more strongly than ever. The truth is, Fred told us later, he had never stopped thinking about his daughter. So, while killing some time between appointments in his hotel room one day, he started flipping through the yellow pages and came to an advertisement for 'Research Etc., ...*adoption reunion specialists.*' Before he realized it, he had dialed our number. This telephone call changed his life.

Fred had previously tried to find his birthdaughter on his own, by joining an adoption search and support group, and by placing ads in Phoenix newspapers, but that method had turned up nothing. He was discouraged, but deep down he had never given up the hope of one day finding the daughter he had relinquished so many years ago.

We are always on alert when we take on a case to make sure that a potential client has good intentions in tracking down birth relatives. And because a birthfather initiating a search without the birthmother involved was pretty rare, we were extra cautious with Fred, so we arranged to meet him in person.

It became very clear to us from our first meeting that Fred was just a very kind, open and sincere man. It was easy for us to sympathize with him. We were touched by his honesty and his feelings about his birthdaughter and we were eager to help him.

Here's Fred's story in his own words:

> "I was pretty much of a drifter at age 26 with a real fear of commitment when my girlfriend, Jan, became pregnant. Keeping the baby was out of the question for us and we decided the best thing to do was place the baby for adoption. While we made the decision together, in retrospect, I see now that I was a bit more coercive about the decision.
>
> "Jan and I married soon after we discovered she was pregnant, but we still kept with our plan for adoption with Family Service Agency. We placed our baby with an agency because it seemed so much safer to us.

"We told only my mother that Jan was pregnant—but when the baby was actually born, I told her there was a miscarriage. We were scared and no one else ever knew the truth.

"We stayed in our apartment during Jan's pregnancy and later rented a small house. I was curious about the adoptive parents, but was not given any information about them. The adoption process was very secretive and the case-workers and hospital personnel didn't really relate to me. We were not given any of the legal papers from the adoption proceedings. Although I never discussed it with the Family Service Agency, I think they may have talked with Jan about what type of family she wanted the baby placed with.

"Throughout the years that followed, I thought of my birthdaughter often, often, often! How was she? Did she have a happy life? Were her adoptive parents good to her? After my birthdaughter turned 21, I decided to initiate a search for her. First, I placed ads in the newspapers in the city where she was born. Several search groups contacted me and I heard from three searching adoptees, none of whom were my birthdaughter."

A Birthmother's Trauma

At our first meeting, Fred told us that he and Jan had divorced shortly after the baby was born, but they still kept in touch occasionally. Interestingly enough, Jan wanted nothing to do with finding their adult birthdaughter. When Fred first started searching, he called Jan, who was helpful about sharing what information she had, along with her family medical history of cancer that she felt her birthdaughter should know about; however, she was adamant that she wanted no personal involvement whatsoever.

It might be tempting for some to judge her as being hard and unfeeling, but the opposite is probably closer to the truth. At the time of the relinquishment, Jan was likely much more traumatized than Fred. We know, from conversations with Fred, that she spent years in therapy trying to gain some emotional distance from the event. So the thought of revisiting it all over again was probably just too much for her to face.

A Birthfather's Reflections

> "I was not prepared for Jan's total resistance to helping me search for our birthdaughter and the subsequent reunion. I now know that she was traumatized by giving up our baby and she has been through therapy to help put it all behind her. I believe that, back then, she thought that if she kept our baby, sooner or later I would abandon her to a life as a single mother. All of this has made me realize what a jerk I was at the age of 26."

Jan helped Fred by giving him the NIDI that was provided to her by the adoption agency regarding the adoptive family. This information contained the first names and dates of birth of the adoptive parents. Fred had also kept the hospital bill from 1965 showing the three-day stay that cost them only $189.60.

The Adverse Adoptive Parents

The adoptive parents' first names were a bit unusual and using the limited database resources we had at the time, we were able to track down a couple named Gustavus and Ramona that we believed to be the adoptive parents.

This couple now resided in Gilroy, California, and Kristen called them to verify that they were the adoptive parents we were looking for. Gustavus answered the phone call, and after identifying herself, Kristen asked if he and his wife had adopted a daughter who was born on the date listed on the hospital record. Understandably, he was less than cordial, but admitted that indeed they had; however, he wouldn't give any more information than that, since he said he couldn't be sure who Kristen really was.

Kristen encouraged Gustavus to verify our license and legitimacy with the Arizona Department of Public Safety and informed him that he could visit our website for more information about our company, but he was reluctant. He talked aside to his wife several times during the phone conversation, and finally said he needed some confirmation that Kristen was indeed representing his daughter's birthparents.

Kristen called him a few times after that with more identifying information, but he refused to tell his daughter that her birthfather was looking for her. Kristen could see they were going nowhere, so she called the adoption agency and told them she was working with a man who believed he was the birthfather of a particular adoptee who was placed through their agency. Kristen told the case worker that she was certain they were a match, but the two individuals wanted absolute confirmation.

The case worker informed Kristen that the agency needed signed letters requesting the confirmation from both parties—the birthfather and the adult adoptee—and once they received signed letters, they would review the file and confirm if they were a match.

Once again, Kristen called Gustavus and explained to him that in order for him to get the confirmation he wanted, he would have to tell his daughter about our having contacted him. He would have to involve her in this because the letter to the adoption agency had to come from her since she was an adult.

Well, Gustavus didn't want to do this either. He flatly refused to tell his daughter that her birthfather was reaching out to her. We felt a sense of sympathy for him and his wife. It's not unusual for parents to feel threatened. Adoptive parents generally do not think of their child as their 'adopted child' and can sort of 'forget' over the years that their child was adopted, so contact from the birthparents can be a shock to them.

As kindly and politely as she could, Kristen explained to Gustavus that the fact was, that since his daughter Cindy was an adult, she had the right to know that a man who could be her birthfather was reaching out to her. It should be Cindy's decision on how to proceed, and her choice to meet her birthparents or not. And Kristen added:

> "Gustavus, I already have Cindy's current address. I can send her a letter directly myself, but I just felt it may be easier for her to hear it from you. Would you please just give her a message to call me?"

Finally, Gustavus and Ramona agreed to contact their daughter on our behalf.

Sometimes, when adoptive parents are resistant to their adult child searching for or being found by a birthparent, it can be because they are fearful that their standing as parents could be changed. Although this is often their main worry, and one we've heard over and over, it is usually completely unfounded. It's a very rare case to find someone who is actually looking to replace their parents[2]—especially once they are adults! The parents may also be afraid of bringing an 'unknown' into their family's world—a fear that this person could even reject their child completely, or in some way bring discord or upheaval into their lives. We have also seen many cases where the adoptive parents almost 'adopt' the birthmother, who is usually much younger than they are, into their family and lives. Such parents figure that this woman carried their child and gave them a precious gift, why shouldn't they welcome knowing her and want their adult child to experience meeting her, or even sharing in her life?

We've been told by some adoptive parents that they want to be there for their adult child to provide emotional support in case the reunion doesn't go well. We find that when the adoptive parents are

---

2 The only case we've had where an adoptee was actually seeking out her birthmother because she needed a mother is included in this book. (Trinity's Story).

supportive, their adult child can face anything. Together they can share in the excitement of the search and the anticipation of reunion. If the search outcome is disappointing, an adoptee can always turn to supportive parents for comfort. When a search has a disappointing outcome, such as a birthparent denying contact or being found deceased, the pain can be eased, by having the honest support of parents. A hug and reassurance that "I am so sorry, I am here for whatever you need" won't make the heartache of rejection or disappointment go away, but at least it won't worsen it by the adoptee feeling a double rejection. However, when adoptive parents strongly oppose a search and/or reunion, and if it goes badly, the adoptee has no one to fall back on. All they may get from their parents is an 'I told you so,' or sometimes just a silent disapproval that may be interpreted by the adoptee as, 'Well, you got what you deserved for being so disloyal to your family.'

The Agreeable Birth Daughter

A day or two later, Cindy called our office and we explained the situation to her. We told her we were pretty sure that our client was her birthfather, and explained the procedure for getting positive confirmation from the adoption agency. We also asked her if she would be interested in having contact with her birthfather after we received positive confirmation from the agency.

Cindy was pretty laid-back about the whole thing. Very composed, she calmly told us that, yes, she'd be interested in having contact with her birthfather. She sent in her request to the adoption agency and they matched it up with Fred's request and, sure enough, they were a match!

While Cindy was cool, calm and collected, Fred was ecstatic!

> "When Research Etc. called and told me that they had found my birthdaughter, Cindy, I felt nothing but delightful panic! After many phone calls, letters and photos back and forth, my birthdaughter and I met at a family reunion in my hometown of Raleigh, North Carolina. She met the whole family.
>
> "We're planning another meeting soon. Cindy has been totally accepted into my family, which is pretty large. She and my nephews and nieces call each other 'Cuz' and they correspond regularly. Cindy has been especially kind to my 87 year old mother—something that means the world to me."

Of course, Fred had to confess to his mother that there had never been a miscarriage at all—and here was the daughter to prove it. Fred's mother was just happy to get to know her granddaughter, and couldn't have cared less about her son's earlier deception.

When Cindy arrived in Raleigh for the family reunion, a funny thing happened on the way to the hotel where she was going to stay. She was met at the airport by two carloads of newly found and over-enthusiastic cousins. Perhaps because of everyone's excitement at being together, they had a hard time locating the hotel. They drove around for a long time before finally spotting it, but then they couldn't figure out how to actually get to it from the freeway they were on. Finally they pulled over to discuss their predicament, and her cousins decided the best thing would be for Cindy to just come stay with them. By this time Cindy felt very comfortable with them, so she called the hotel and canceled her reservation and went home to stay with her new cousins.

Flesh of My Flesh

Cindy told Fred that she had known she was adopted from a young age and that she'd always felt like she wasn't related to another soul on the face of the earth. She would love to have contact with her birthmother, but she says that being a woman, she can understand why Jan has chosen to remain separate.

As for Fred, he recently told Kristen,

> "Finding Cindy changed everything for me. Suddenly I knew; '*here she is.*' It was not a matter of ego, but a matter of her being the flesh of my flesh."

Fred lost his own father in WWII when he was seven. He felt that maybe it was possible that because of that traumatic loss, he had never felt very rooted himself, and so opted to relinquish his daughter to adoption. Or maybe he feared his daughter would lose him the way he lost his own father. In any case, he's made every effort to make things right today. He acknowledges, with gratitude, that the father who raised her will always be her father, but he and Cindy will always have a connection that cannot be broken.

> "I am very much in favor for being able to connect with one's adult birth children," Fred says. "Beyond just simple health records, I feel there is a very real need to know. My feelings have not changed over the years. I'm struck by how few birthfathers come to the adoption support group meetings. I think that when I attend, I help serve as evidence that not all birthfathers are two-headed monsters denying the consequences of our actions."

CHAPTER 7

Trinity's Search

Opening the Book of Secrets

When adoptees come to us wanting to reconnect with their birthparents, usually they're craving answers to who they are and where they've come from. Or sometimes they only want or need medical history. Amazingly, in almost every case, they are not looking for a *mother.* This is because they already have a mother, and a father for that matter, in the form of their adoptive family. But Trinity was different. Trinity came to us in dire need of a mother.

Trinity had the misfortune of being adopted by parents that really didn't want her. In our experience, this is very rare. Usually when parents adopt children, it's because they dearly want them. Parents, adoptive or not, may have personality flaws or other issues that can cause friction between them and their children, but usually, it does not stem from a lack of wanting or loving their child.

Trinity's situation was different, and for her, extremely painful. Acting out of greed, not love or a desire to be parents, Trinity's prospective adoptive parents were pursuing a family fortune promised by her father's parents to the one of their offspring that had the most children. Unable to conceive naturally, Trinity's parents ultimately adopted four children, with Trinity being the youngest, and they won the inheritance.

Trinity and her adoptive siblings grew up in an environment of tremendous financial wealth—million dollar homes, nannies, maids, cooks and chauffeurs, etc.—but also in an environment of profound emotional poverty. While their wealthy and self-centered parents jet-setted around the world, the children were left to be raised by nannies. They knew from the start that they were adopted by two strangers, and it felt to them that their mansion was more like an orphanage than a real home.

This was not easy for Trinity to talk about:

> "I had to draw upon some very painful memories, face a few buried ghosts, and try to give words to feelings that I still don't even understand... I had to think of what this child inside me felt. If I lied or made it seem less than it was, I'd be barring her again, telling her to hide, telling her that she is not important, that her feelings are not real."

This neglectful situation lasted until Trinity's father died in 1972 when she was 8 years old. By this time, her mother, who, in any case, cannot be said to have ever cared for any of them, was too mentally unstable to be responsible for the four children. Their care and upbringing was entrusted entirely to the current nanny, Lila, who already treated the children as her own.

The Stork's Mistake

Trinity remembered being asked to create a family tree in elementary school. Since her adoptive father was dead and her adoptive mother wanted nothing to do with her, Trinity listed Nanny Lila as her mother. The teacher told her she couldn't do that, because Lila was not her blood relative. Since Trinity didn't know of any *blood* relatives to put on her tree—she felt totally confused and completely alone in the world.

> "It was as if the stork had made a huge mistake, made one too many babies for that day and just dropped me, hoping no one would notice."

This sense of not belonging anywhere stuck with Trinity throughout her childhood, and even into young adulthood. Trinity fell in love and married, and she and her husband adopted three children in the first years of their marriage. It wasn't until Trinity had a biological daughter of her own that she found the courage to look for answers and seek out her birthmother. Her story made us very anxious to help her.

> "My daughter's birth brought up feelings and thoughts from long ago. I realized that I'd been searching since the day I was taken away from that hospital by my adoptive parents. I had kept the names of my adopted children's birthparents as I wanted them to know everything about their medical histories and ethnic backgrounds. It was only fair that my biological child should have the same opportunity. I never wanted ANY of my children to feel the emptiness and sense of abandonment that I had experienced."

The Waiting Game

Trinity began poking around looking for information about her birthmother, but soon discovered there were many obstacles in her way. Most of the people who might have been involved had died, and her adoptive mother (whom she had not heard from in almost 24 years) refused to even speak to her over the phone. Though Nanny had no information about her birthparents, she made it perfectly clear that she was unhappy about Trinity's search and tried to dissuade her from continuing her search:

> "She told me I'd ruin my birthparents' lives if I was to appear, that they had given me up and that meant they wouldn't want me to find them."

It is to Trinity's credit that her determination and drive did not allow her nanny's opinion, or any of the obstacles in her way, to stop her from trying to find some of the answers to the questions that had plagued her throughout her life. Trinity decided to seek out professional help. She contacted Kristen through the CIP.

After hearing her story, Kristen agreed to become her guide through what was clearly going to be a complicated and emotionally challenging journey. Trinity later said:

> "Kristen was very straightforward with me. She didn't fill my head with false promises, but after our conversation, I had hope, something I had never dared to feel before."

After Trinity filled out the CIP paperwork, the waiting game began. Trinity recalls getting through this period of limbo on autopilot. At the same time she was waiting to hear any news about the progress of her search, her marriage was in turmoil, her children were sick and needed her love and attention, and to top it off, her adoptive mother died. She managed it all, but felt as though she was going through the motions without really feeling any of it. During the wait, she recalls how she coped with her feelings of rejection:

> "For part of my adult life I believed that I must have been kidnapped from my birthparents. This helped me feel less unwanted, because of course, they must have loved me, but I had been stolen and what could they have done? In this fantasy of mine, they were heartbroken and I was able to cry for their loss."

To emphasize just how real the rejection was, it was discovered that even though Trinity was well taken care of financially by her adoptive parents, she was not even mentioned in either of their obituaries.

Reunion—One Step at a Time

The search began with Trinity's adoption file. It had been a private adoption and the file gave almost no information. It did offer a name, though no age, for Trinity's birthmother. After running a name search on a private database, one match was found. The discovery led to a very kind widower living in Queens, New York, who helped us with enough information about his recently deceased wife that it was plain that there was no way his wife could have been Trinity's birthmother—at the time of Trinity's birth, the couple had been living in Germany where he was working in the military. It was back to the drawing board.

At the time an adoption is finalized, an adoptee's original birth certificate is sealed and they are issued a new birth certificate, often referred to as an 'amended birth certificate.' An amended birth certificate reflects the name given to the adoptee by the adoptive parents, the adoptive parents' names, ages and addresses. It is made to look as if the adoptee is the natural child born to the adoptive parents. Because it was necessary for Kristen to find Trinity's birthmother's maiden name and other essential information, Kristen obtained a court order to unseal Trinity's original birth certificate.

This key document provided Trinity's birthmother's date of birth, age, place of birth and maiden name. We found out she was in her early twenties at the time of Trinity's birth. The year was 1964, the place, Tempe, Arizona. Her maiden name was Loretta Smith.

Using the 1964 city directory for Tempe, Kristen found a Loretta Smith listed at an apartment address. The directory also listed her occupation and employer—she had been a secretary for a large electronics company. Kristen also discovered from the listing she was single, living on her own.

It was now 1995 and time to locate and make contact with Loretta. Using her date of birth, first name and maiden name, we ran database searches until we identified her and found her current address. Kristen found out that she went by the nickname of 'Lettie.'

Panic at First Contact

Kristen called Lettie in Winter Haven, Florida, and introduced herself as a CI and explained about the CIP. Lettie was so completely silent that Kristen was sure she'd stopped breathing. Kristen asked her if she was Loretta Smith. Lettie flat out denied it. Kristen asked if she had worked for a certain electronics company in 1964. "No," again. It was *'No'* to every question Kristen asked.

Finally, Lettie said, "Don't ever call me again!" and slammed down the phone. Kristen still remembers how horrible she felt when this happened:

> "I was completely devastated. This was the first case I had taken as a CI, and although I had plenty of experience with adoption searches as a PI, I wanted to do my very best to give all parties a happy outcome using this special program. All I could think of was how terrible this was going to be for Trinity. I knew how much this meant to her and how much of herself she had invested in finding this woman. I took it as a personal failure on my part—I wanted so much for this to work out for Trinity."

Kristin dreaded the call she would have to make to Trinity, but bit the bullet and made the call. Kristen told her what had happened, that the woman had denied all knowledge of a daughter and had hung up on her. According to the rules of the CIP, Kristen only had one more chance of re-contacting Lettie, and then, if Lettie refused again, Trinity would be required to wait a whole year before Kristen could try to contact her again. Kristen told Trinity that it would be best to wait a few weeks before she called again. Kristen also explained that she had managed to get out the name of the Confidential Intermediary Program, as well as her own name, before Lettie hung up, but there was no opportunity to give a contact number. Kristen felt sure this was Trinity's birthmother and told her so. The affect on Trinity was understandably intense, as she later told Kristen:

> "I was physically trembling inside. The years of fear and rejection built up in me, smothering me, and tears began to flow from my eyes. I made Kristen repeat everything. I kept asking and re-asking, feeling as though I wasn't hearing any of it right."

Coming this close to her birthmother and then being denied was especially tough. "But did you tell her how much I *need* her?" she asked, crying. Kristen had to admit that she simply hadn't had a chance, because Lettie had hung up so abruptly.

Kristen remembers:

> "Trinity told me that I *had* to call back—she said that she needed her mother. This is a very rare thing for me to hear. Mostly, the people who come to us really aren't looking for another mother. But with Trinity, she'd never had one. Her neediness and the sheer desperation in her voice moved me to keep going. My heart broke for her. I wasn't totally sure what approach I would take, but knew I needed to wait a while to give Lettie some breathing room and a little time to digest my initial call."

Trinity admitted that though she had never openly allowed herself to hope, she now had to face the fact that deep inside, she had *more* than hoped. For decades she had dreamed, wished, prayed and begged for a mother. It was as though the whole world was watching the child inside her, and everybody finally knew once and for all that she was not good enough to be loved. Tormenting thoughts ran through her mind:

> "Is this really happening? What about my medical history? Could she be so heartless, doesn't she want to know I'm okay? Even the one who gave birth to me can't acknowledge my existence? Have I really come this close to have it all snatched away?"

A Mother Reconsiders

After two weeks, Kristen called Lettie back and the minute she heard Lettie's voice, she quickly asked her to please not hang up. Now it was Lettie's turn to let it all out. She told Kristen she wasn't going to hang up, that she'd been frantic, trying to remember the name of the agency program for the past two weeks, and that she had panicked when Kristen first called, and had become overwhelmed with fear. Apparently, no one in her life knew anything about Trinity. Lettie confided that she had an adult son, Jerry, that had been born before Trinity and he knew nothing about her existence. Lettie had a lot of close friends and they, too, had never been told about this period of her life.

Sometimes it just makes sense to hold back, and because of her experience, Kristen knew just what to say and what not to say. She decided it was not her place to tell Lettie at that point, that her birthdaughter had had a traumatic upbringing. It would have only made Lettie feel worse about relinquishing her birthdaughter if she found out she'd been placed in a loveless, emotionally neglectful family and could have cast a shadow over their first meeting. Kristen knew that it was up to Trinity when, and even whether, to divulge this kind of personal information. Instead, Kristen told Lettie that Trinity's adoptive parents were both deceased and that Trinity had been given a financially privileged childhood and had even adopted children herself.

Lettie told Kristen that at the time of the adoption, she had been very curious about the people who were going to take her baby. She was told they were very wealthy and that the mother wasn't able to conceive. That was all. No paperwork exchanged hands and she now saw how naïve she had been.

The pregnancy had come at a terrible time for Lettie, and the tough decisions she had to make were a heavy burden for her to bear alone, as she explained:

> "I was 23 when I gave birth to my daughter. I was divorced and had a son, Trinity's half brother, and it was hard enough trying to raise him on my own. When I got pregnant with her, I had to stop work and go on welfare. I had a girlfriend in the same situation as mine, and we moved in together to share living expenses. I knew in my heart that this child would be better off with a family that could afford to give her a life I knew I wouldn't be able to. I'd only gone as far as the ninth grade in school and it was all I could do to keep me and my son going with the secretarial jobs I could get. Trinity's father had no idea of my decision, he'd left the state and I had no way of contacting him. I didn't tell anyone about my pregnancy. My family had no idea."

The next step toward facilitating full contact was to send Lettie a form to sign and have notarized in order to release her contact information. Because Trinity had initiated the search, it was up to her to make the first call. In the meantime, Kristen was thrilled to call Trinity and let her know that her birthmother had changed her mind and was excited to meet with her. As Kristen filled her in on the details of why her birthmother had hung up and how she felt now, she also informed Trinity that she had an older half brother and that her birthmother was planning on telling him about her.

Reunion Do's and Don'ts

When Trinity hung up from this conversation, she didn't know what to feel. She cried, she laughed. But mostly, she decided to keep the good news all to herself for a while. She didn't want anyone spoiling the wonderful feelings inside.

It was some time before she shared the news with her siblings and Nanny. Unable to contain her excitement any longer, she began to share her happy news with everybody. She was met with many different reactions, in addition to all of the emotions going on in her own self. Waiting for the consent forms seemed to take forever and Trinity remained on pins and needles, fearing her birthmother would change her mind.

We advised both Trinity and Lettie of topics of conversation to avoid on first contact. We suggested that Trinity didn't just dive right into the question of, 'Why did you relinquish me?' We also told her to try to avoid mentioning her birthfather straight away, unless Lettie brought it up first. These core issues always come up later anyhow, and in our experience, it's better to keep things light and flowing the first time. Topics like: 'What are your hobbies, what were your favorite subjects in school, what is your profession,' and so on. It's important to have ideas in your head before you talk so that you avoid having the conversation go 'dead.' Everyone has experienced a lull in a conversation, when both parties are scrambling to think of something to say. This can be awkward even in casual conversation; much less in talking to someone you may have waited your entire life to talk to!

It's important to prepare some things to talk about in advance, in the likely event that the realization hits you that you are actually speaking with the one person who has remained a mystery until now, so that you are not suddenly rendered speechless.

Opening the Book of Secrets

The first telephone conversation was initially awkward. Lettie and Trinity were both bundles of nerves with so much to say and share. They didn't speak about the adoption, and Trinity answered Lettie's questions about her children and her life. Their conversation ended years of wondering for both of them. "Even though we had not yet met face to face," Trinity says, "I felt a sense of belonging for the first time in my life."

Lettie's experience was similar:

> "When my daughter called me it was strained at first but as we talked, I felt as though she had been with me forever, we had so much to catch up on and then she decided to plan to fly from another state to meet me as soon as possible."

Trinity talked with her half brother, Jerry, as well. His excitement was contagious. In the conversation, they learned that they both were going to be in Los Angeles for business the next week, and decided to take the plunge and meet up. During this conversation he called her 'Sister' and told her how he had wished for a brother or sister his whole life. He assured her that their mother wanted to meet her more than anything.

In Los Angeles they booked into the same hotel and had dinner together and talked for several hours. Both had a lot of questions. Trinity wanted to know what it had been like to be raised by Lettie, and Jerry told her as much as he could. This meeting meant the world to Trinity, and she later told us:

> "It was like opening a secret book and not wanting to stop reading until the end. We hugged and made promises to keep in touch. He wished me luck as the next day was my long-awaited meeting in Florida with our birthmother."

Trinity flew to Florida with her husband and two of the children, their seven-year-old daughter and 18-month-old baby. Despite their support and companionship, she remembers feeling alone and very frightened. In the car, she gave the wrong directions and got them lost in Winter Haven. When they finally found the right street, she ended up knocking at a neighbor's house in instead of her birthmother's. Finally, when they were standing in front of the right door, Trinity's heart was pounding and she was sure it was so loud that all the neighbors could hear. She later told us:

> "From the moment she opened the door, I knew I had found home. We spent a couple of days together, sharing photo albums, tears, and many stories. We cooked dinners and discovered we had similar tastes in most things. I learned about my medical background, and things fell into place, things that would help my biological daughter."

When it was time for Trinity and her family to leave, Lettie held her tight. A word Trinity had never used before slipped through her lips, and it felt so right, so natural:

> "I didn't have to think about it and as I heard it, my heart stopped. The word was 'Mom.' I was scared about how she would react to it, would she even want that role? I still have the warm feeling she gave me. So, with tears in our eyes, we parted and made promises for our future together, without expectations."

Eventually, Trinity and her husband divorced, and she moved with her children to Florida to be near Lettie. The two women became firm friends and even fell into the usual mother-daughter conflicts, almost as though Lettie and Trinity had not been separated all those years. Through this experience Trinity finally created a sense of family for herself and Lettie is thrilled to have a larger family to share with and enjoy.

Lettie tells us:

> "There are still so many things to learn about each other but I love her as much as I love my son. Having her and all her children, my grandchildren, has been such a blessing. And it hasn't changed my relationship with other family members."

Lettie highly recommends to anyone who has placed a child for adoption or for an adult adoptee to follow their desire to search out and find their adult birth child or parent. She also feels that it is the adult adoptees' right to know their history, not only for medical reasons but for emotional ones too.

No More Secrets

After a time, this family's book of secrets opened up even more. Lettie confessed to Trinity, and to us, that she had placed another child for adoption—a son. This baby boy was born before Trinity, when Lettie was nineteen. At the time she discovered she was pregnant, Lettie was living with her mother and stepfather. Lettie's mother told her that they were going to 'get rid of it.' They tried several things, from Lettie sitting on a stool and her mother pulling it out from under her, to hot mustard baths. Of course, none of these methods worked. Lettie remembers:

> "In the end I was sent to Texas to a home for unwed girls. Once my son was born, they took him away and it was only two weeks later that I was allowed to hold him. They gave me papers to sign and that was the last I saw of him."

She asked us if we would try to locate him. We got to work using the boy's date of birth and first name in order to track him down. Within a week, we'd located Lettie's birthson, Louis, in North Carolina. Ava called and found him to be a soft-spoken, kind man. Sadly, Louis' adoptive mother had very recently passed away and he just wasn't emotionally prepared to meet in person with Lettie and his half-siblings, Jerry and Trinity. Several days passed before he called them, and they all spoke to each other and shared stories. Though Lettie was eager to build a relationship with him, together with her other children, Louis was not ready to take that step. Lettie understands his feelings and says:

> "I still send birthday and Christmas cards but don't receive any back. I think he is just so involved in his life that we don't come to mind very often. He did thank me once for giving him life which I thought was a wonderful thing to do. Finding him has helped me put an end to some of the questions I had over the years."

Today Trinity and Lettie enjoy a close relationship. Because of their coming together, two of Trinity's adoptive siblings were inspired to search out their birthparents, and we feel privileged to be able to help them to find closure in their lives, just as Trinity did.

Because of the emotional involvement we have with some of our clients, a working relationship has occasionally turned to one of friendship. Such was the case with Trinity and Lettie. Both women have visited at Kristen's home, shared dinner at a restaurant and keep in touch with phone calls. Judy, Ava and Kristen were honored to be invited to share in the joyous occasion of Trinity's wedding several years after the reunion.

Kristen recalls:

> "It was so amazing to see Trinity, glowing and radiant, with her new husband and her entire family, finally complete. The wedding and reception took place in Trinity's sprawling, family-oriented home. Lettie and Jerry were there, along with Louis and his family who flew in from North Carolina, Trinity's children (who all took part in the wedding ceremony), Trinity's siblings, Nanny—and even her ex-husband! I'll never forget looking around the room and being overcome by the realization that I was witnessing Trinity's lifelong dream come true, right before my eyes. I was not only witnessing it, I was also a part of it. This realization was such a gift to me that I can honestly say this is the true reward of our work; bringing people together and seeing them come to a place of

understanding and acceptance. I feel personally blessed to have had Trinity and Lettie brought into my life—initially as clients, now as friends."

Some final words from Trinity:

"I believe in my heart that my mother needed me as much as I needed her. And all those around us have only benefited from our finding each other."

CHAPTER 8

Steven's Search

From Fear to Healing

Some of our most interesting cases have come by way of the Arizona Confidential Intermediary Program (CIP), for which Kristen served as a certified Confidential Intermediary (CI). The CIP is operated by the Arizona Supreme Court, and the trained intermediaries have access to sealed adoption records when hired by an Arizona adoptee, birth parent, or sibling. The CI uses that confidential information to locate and help facilitate reunions, or the exchange of vital information between the triad members. The Confidential Intermediary program is a very fair and practical way to initiate an adoption search because it protects the privacy of all involved individuals, and offers an affordable search option.

Steven, of Native American heritage, can only be described as a tall, dark, and handsome gentle giant of a man. At age 31, he had finally worked up the courage to search for his birthmother. He was living in California with his adoptive father at the time, but because his adoption had occurred in Arizona, he contacted the CIP, got a list of the CI's and chose Kristen to work with.

Kristen recalls that her initial conversations with Steven were somewhat different than the conversations she'd had with other clients. Usually, an adoptee embarking on a search is full of questions and hours can be spent going over how the search process works, what the possible outcomes can be, and generally discussing the feelings and fears that can arise during the process. It struck Kristen that Steven didn't ask many questions at all and he certainly didn't express his feelings about his search one way or the other. While Kristen was puzzled by his lack of emotion or enthusiasm, she suspected that perhaps Steven was just too afraid to get his hopes up for fear they would be dashed. It was only after Steven opened up to contribute his experiences for this book, that Kristen's suspicions were confirmed. Still waters often run very deep and that was definitely the case with Steven.

Steven later recalled what he was feeling leading up to the search:

> "I was very young when my mother told me that I was adopted. I have always carried with me a sense of rejection in knowing that I was adopted. I never looked like anyone in my adoptive family and I always wondered whom I looked like. I also suffered with an extremely painful foot condition, gout, which is a pretty uncommon ailment for a young man to be plagued with and I always wondered if it was an inherited illness."

Steven listened silently as Kristen explained the various scenarios that could occur once she found his birthmother: His birthmother might agree to full contact. If she didn't want full contact, she might be willing to exchange non-identifying letters. This could include medical background, so at least he might be able to determine if the gout came from her side of the family. The CIP does not allow for a CI to divulge any information to either party without a signed consent form from both parties. If Steven's birthmother decided to deny either full or non-identifying contact, the search would be over without any release of information—and Steven's only option would be to wait at least a year and then have Kristen re-contact her in case she had had a change of heart. Steven could not even know what state his birthmother lived in—the CIP is literally that confidential.

Facing His Fears

For someone like Steven, who already had a feeling of not exactly fitting in physically with his adoptive family, this process brought him face to face with his worst fear: rejection by the woman who had brought him into this world. It took great determination on his part not to go back on his desire to reconnect with his birthmother. As Steven puts it:

> "Because I had spent years of feeling rejected, I set myself up to believe that my birthmother would automatically deny contact with me. I wouldn't let myself get overly excited thinking about the fact that she might actually want to know me, but deep down, I held on to some small hope that she would."

Although it wasn't easy for Steven emotionally, the actual search for his birthmother turned out to be a breeze. Kristen was able to obtain her maiden name and date of birth from the court papers. It turned out that her name, Paulietta, was so rare that only one came up in our private investigation databases for the whole country, and she was the right age. Kristen knew she had identified Steven's birthmother.

The next step was to tell Steven the news. Despite how quickly Kristen had found his birthmother, he was still keeping his expectations low. As he puts it:

> "I asked Kristen to tell my birthmother that I did not want to cause her any upset nor did I want to intrude

> on her life. I did want her to know I was alive and well, however, and I would really appreciate her giving me some non-identifying medical history, especially because of my ongoing problem with gout. I was positive that my birthmother would not want contact with me, so I felt the best I could hope for was a non-identifying letter."

Kristen was unable to find a telephone number for Paulietta, but because she lived in such a small community, Kristen contacted the local postmaster and asked for his help in locating her. The Postmaster was very cordial, didn't ask questions and didn't hesitate to help. He didn't have a phone number for Paulietta, but he did have one for her sister, Irene, and he freely gave it to Kristen.

Kristen called Paulietta's sister and found her at home. Kristen didn't divulge the reason for her call to Irene, she only stressed to her that it was very important that Paulietta call her. Kristen had a feeling, by the way Irene responded, that she knew exactly what this call was really about. It almost seemed as if, after three decades, the family was just waiting for a sign of life from the son who had been separated from them.

Pins and Needles

It wasn't long before Paulietta herself called the office. When Kristen explained who she was and why she had called, Paulietta nearly burst with excitement. Kristen went on to explain that if Paulietta wasn't ready for full contact, Steven would appreciate a non-identifying letter containing some medical history, and the first thing out of her mouth was: "Tell him that *gout* runs in our family!" Kristen couldn't contain herself and blurted out, "He has gout, too!" Of course, by now it was evident that Paulietta was more than willing to have full contact with her birthson.

Later, Paulietta wrote:

> "I was stunned and completely overwhelmed with emotion. After 31 long years my son had come looking for me! I couldn't wait to tell everyone that he was okay and he had found us!"

Paulietta couldn't get the words out fast enough—she began by giving Kristen all the best times for her birthson to call her. She even told Kristen when her bowling night was because she wouldn't be home then. Paulietta was so beside herself with excitement that Kristen hated to have to cut short her sheer joy by informing her of the fact that there was a procedure that must be followed by the CIP before any identifying information could be released between either of them. Paulietta first would have to sign and return a notarized form to be filed with the Arizona Supreme Court, just as Steven had already done. It could take a few days via mail.

Meanwhile, Steven was feeling extremely anxious to know what was going on:

> "I was on pins and needles waiting for her (Kristen) to call me back and give me the bad news. When the phone rang, I knew right away, by the sound of Kristen's voice, that contact with my birthmother had been made and something positive had happened. Something positive had happened, alright! In spite of my fear, my birthmother actually wanted to have full contact with me! It took a few minutes for the words I was hearing to register. She actually wanted to know me!"

Answered Prayers

Once we received Paulietta's notarized form, Kristen was legally allowed to exchange contact information between Steven and Paulietta. She set up the agreed upon time Steven would call Paulietta, gave them both a few pointers on first contacts, and made Steven promise to call the next day and tell us all about it! Steven tells what happened next:

> "I called Paulietta and we talked for a long time. She told me that her whole family was anxiously waiting to meet me. We made arrangements for me to fly from California to Arizona to meet her. I couldn't believe this was all happening so fast, and I was so scared I didn't know what to do! When I arrived at Paulietta's house in Arizona, there was a whole group of people, all birth relatives, waiting for me—a whole group of people that looked just like me! Seeing all of them and getting to know each person gave me the sense that I finally knew where I belonged."

Paulietta was thrilled with the reunion as well:

> "We talked for our very first time on October 10, 1998. We made plans for him to come to Arizona for the Thanksgiving weekend. I would finally be able to hug my oldest son and my boys would finally be able to know their older brother. When the time came, I picked him up at the airport and brought him to my home. My whole family welcomed Steven and we spent a wonderful weekend getting to know one another. He looks so much like my other sons and I am sure he saw the resemblance, too!"

From Fear to Healing

Steven and Paulietta's reunion is the kind of result that has made our work so rewarding over the years. It's also why we're strongly in favor of reunions when they are handled correctly. There are many different opinions about whether birth families should be reunited at all. For a long time, the prominent belief was that separation through adoption should be accepted as final, and that the people involved should not try to go back and find one another. But we think that Steven's story, and the stories of so many others, show that reunions can offer a wonderful chance for people to heal old wounds and put less happy times squarely in the past where they belong. Paulietta says:

> "Having Steven in our lives has brought my immediate and extended family even closer together. Being able to reach out to a birth family member is the greatest option we now have. Because of this, my life has been forever changed for the better. I find that I am a much happier person and am finally content. I am so proud that I now have all of my boys to make our family complete!"

A Father's Feelings

When a reunion occurs, it not just the adoptee and birthparents whose lives are impacted. Anyone close to them feels the effect as well. In Steven's case, he was fortunate enough to have a father who helped and supported him all the way. Steven's older brother, Clinton, was also adopted, but never had a desire to reconnect with his birthmother. So when Steven decided he wanted to try and find Paulietta, his father, Jim, had mixed feelings, only because he felt extremely protective of Steven and didn't want to see him get hurt.

Here's how Steven's father Jim felt about the reunion:

> "I was very happy and relieved for Steven when we found out that his birthmother was receptive to contact and wanted to know him. I also spoke to her by phone shortly after they made contact and assured her of my full support in their meeting each other. I supported the idea so much, in fact, that I bought Steven a plane ticket to Arizona to visit her!
>
> "A couple of months later, I invited Paulietta to come to California and stay at my home with us. I was glad that she took me up on the offer and came for a visit. Needless to say, she appeared a little nervous and

> I felt bad about that, as I wanted her to feel comfortable with us and to know that she and her other sons are welcome to visit our home anytime.

"Steven's finding his birthmother has in no way weakened our relationship. We are as close as we have ever been. In fact Steven still lives at home with me and is always welcome to remain as long as he so desires. Steven is a wonderful son and we both love each other very much. Our love for each other is something we have always expressed and continue to do daily."

A Maternal Aunt's Perspective

As Paulietta's older sister, Irene had a uniquely intimate perspective on the events leading up to the adoption, as well as the reunion. During her pregnancy, Paulietta, 18 years old and single, stayed with Irene in Phoenix, to escape the scrutiny of her small town in northern Arizona. Irene recalls their mother being hysterical as she broke the news of Paulietta's predicament. Irene and her husband, Harold, decided that they would take the baby, but their family doctor, whom they consulted, warned against it. The doctor suggested that as surrogate parents of a close relative's baby, they could never be *full* parents to the baby. So, following his advice, it was decided that the best plan was one of adoption outside the family.

Irene worked days while her husband, Harold, worked nights. So when Paulietta went into the hospital, one of them was able to remain with her at all times. As it turned out, Harold was at the hospital when Steven was born. He witnessed a doctor and social worker take the newborn baby out of the nursery room and out a back door of the hospital. He was the last family member to see Steven for the next 31 years.

So when Steven reappeared three decades later, it naturally brought up some concerns for Irene:

> "When I first found out that Paulietta's son had found her, I was stunned. In 1967, when this took place, absolute privacy was guaranteed, and I was always trying to protect Paulietta. I was not about to let her be hurt. Because my mother had died taking this secret to her grave, I was terrified what would happen if my bombastic Dad were told. But when my other sister told him, he just clapped his hands. This is a far cry from the way he felt thirty plus years ago!
>
> "A few months after Steven's first visit with Paulietta, I had the opportunity to meet him on another of his trips through my city to visit with her. Steven calls me Aunt Irene, and we email once in a while. My own children feel I was dead wrong in trying to protect Paulietta from the pain I was afraid she would feel. Most of the family have just accepted the situation as something that happened a long time ago and do not judge it."

A Birth Cousin's Point of View

When Irene's daughter Deanie became pregnant at 21, Paulietta confessed to her young niece about placing her own baby for adoption. Deanie believes Paulietta did this out of a concern that she might be considering abortion as an option, which, Deanie says, hadn't even entered her mind. Although Paulietta had never elaborated much on the subject, Deanie never forgot their conversation, and so Steven's sudden appearance did not come as a complete surprise to her. Deanie recalls Steven's arrival:

> "I was one of the family members who went with Paulietta to the airport to meet Steven. It was so exciting! We were all so nervous waiting for the plane to land, then when it did, we watched as the passengers disembarked. When Steven came down the steps from the

> plane, his brother James said, 'That's him!' I know we overwhelmed him, he was only expecting Paulietta.
>
> "During his 'Welcome Home' reception at Paulietta's house, he just sat in amazement as cousins, aunts, uncles and others seemed to 'crawl out of the woodwork' (as Steven put it) to meet him!
>
> "I think it is great that Steven sought out his birth family. Had he not had the option to seek out his birthmother, so many questions in his own personal life would have remained unanswered. Steven calls Paulietta about once a week, and they always know what's happening in each others' lives. Steven is a truly wonderful and caring person. He is so much like his birthmother it's unreal! I know that having Steven back has made my Aunt feel complete. Her sons gave her a mother's ring which includes Steven's birthstone. She wears it every day."

It's clear to see that while this is Steven's story, it is also very much about the other family members whose lives were touched by this event. Still, since Steven so bravely threw caution to the wind and initiated this search in the face of fear and rejection, we want him to have the last word:

> "I am so thankful that I took this journey in spite of my fears. I finally know where certain traits I've always had come from and knowing Paulietta, my siblings, and the others, has made me realize just how important family really is to me."

Documents

The following pages are some examples of the types of documents we work with to help solve our adoption search cases. These records illustrate the importance of the information provided, which varies from state to state, and from different agencies. Even though they are sometimes very poor quality copies, with some of the information removed or left out, there are still enough clues left in to help us our solve our cases.

SUPERIOR COURT OF CALIFORNIA, COUNTY OF SAN MATEO

IN THE MATTER OF (Minor's Name)
(Full Birth Name) - Birthname
(Full Adopted Name) - Adopted Name

APPLICATION AND ORDER FOR APPROVAL OF THE COURT TO OBTAIN INFORMATION REGARDING AN ADOPTION

Case No.

For the reasons set forth below, permission is hereby sought (check pertinent statement)

_____ to determine whether an action has been filed for the adoption of the party whose name is shown above:

_X_ to obtain a certified copy of decree. Other: Any additional information per the

Other name by which child is known: Federal Indian Child Welfare Act of 1978, s.19

Date of Adoption: 1970-71 Name of adopting parents: (Mother & Father names)

(Family Code 9200 prohibits release of any adoption information "except in exceptional circumstances and for good cause approaching the necessitous".)

REASON FOR REQUEST: Attached is a letter from The Children's Home Society of California, which states tht my birthmother was part Cherokee Indian and that my birthfather was also part American Indian (tribe unknown). Secti 1917 of the Federal Indian Child Welfare Act of 1978 entitles me to know any tribal information, as well as the identity of my biological parents. (See Attached Act).

(If more space is needed use a separate sheet of paper)

(Below give information identifying applicant and relationship to above parties)

Name: Full Adopted Name
Address: Current Address
Relationship: Adoptee/Self
City & State: City, California
Telephone No. Phone Number
Signature: [redacted]
Dated: [redacted]

Subscribed and sworn to before me this day of ______________, 19____. At ______________ California. I certify (or declare under penalty of perjury that the foregoing is true and correct.

[redacted]

SEAL Notary Public Signature

Note: The form of declaration under penalty of perjury to be used only when executed in the State of California. If document is executed outside of State of California, the affidavit form is to be executed before a notary public or other officer authorized to administer oaths.

ORDER

Good cause appearing therefor, permission is hereby granted the above named applicant to obtain the information and the services hereinabove set forth. The Court finds that the requirements of Family Code 9200 have been met.

Dated: ______________

Petition #1 to the Superior Court to Release Records Under the Indian Child Welfare Act of 1978

An example of a Petition for the release of all adoption records held by the court, citing the Indian Child Welfare Act. This particular request was flatly denied in a one-paragraph letter from the presiding judge.

... PLAZA DRIVE
MONTEREY PARK, CA 91754

Superior Court of the State of California, County of Los Angeles

PETITION FOR BIRTH RECORD INFORMATION

Section 10439 Health and Safety Code (Section 102705)

NAME: Adoptee Full Name	DATE OF BIRTH: [illegible]	AGE: 34

PERMANENT RESIDENCE—IN THE COUNTY OF LOS ANGELES, STATE OF CALIFORNIA

STREET: Adoptee Current Address	CITY: [illegible]	ZIP: 90703

I AM INFORMED AND BELIEVE THAT I WAS ADOPTED

BY: Adoptive Mother's Name	IN THE COUNTY OF: Los Angeles, STATE OF CALIFORNIA
AND: Adoptive Father's Name	APPROXIMATE DATE OF ADOPTION: Date of Adoption

OR—I AM INFORMED THAT AN ADOPTION PROCEEDING RELATING TO:

ADOPTEE: Birth Name	BY: Adoptive Mother's Name
WAS COMPLETED IN: LA Superior Court, [illegible] Los Angeles COUNTY, STATE OF CALIFORNIA — APPROXIMATE DATE OF ADOPTION: [illegible]	AND: Adoptive Father's Name — ADOPTIVE PETITIONERS

MY RELATION TO SAID PERSONS IS AS FOLLOWS: (STATE RELATION TO ADOPTEE AND ADOPTIVE PETITIONERS)

Adoptee: Self / Adoptive Petitioners: Adopted Daughter

I REQUEST PERMISSION TO INSPECT THE RECORDS AND OR OBTAIN COPIES OF RECORDS RELATING TO THE BIRTH OF THE NAMED PERSON FOR THE FOLLOWING REASONS: (SECTION 10439 HEALTH AND SAFETY CODE REQUIRES "GOOD AND COMPELLING CAUSE"

IN ORDER TO PROVE MY AMERICAN INDIAN HERITAGE AND THEREFORE BE ABLE TO CLAIM THE BENEFITS I AM ENTITLED TO UNDER FEDERAL LAW.

WHEREFORE, I REQUEST AN ORDER OF THE SUPERIOR COURT AS REQUIRED BY SECTION 10439 OF THE HEALTH AND SAFETY CODE WITH RESPECT TO THE RECORDS RELATING TO THE ABOVE PROCEEDING.

[illegible]
(SIGNATURE)

VERIFICATION

STATE OF CALIFORNIA)
COUNTY OF LOS ANGELES) SS.

I am the Petitioner in the above matter; I have read the foregoing Petition and know the contents thereof; I declare that the same is true of my own knowledge, except as to those matters which are therein stated upon my information and belief, and as to those matters I believe it to be true.

I declare under penalty of perjury under the laws of the State of California that the foregoing is true and correct.

Dated this 2 day of July, 1998 at [illegible], California
(LOCATION)

[illegible]
(SIGNATURE)

138/T7-92

Petition #2 to the Superior Court to Release Records Under the Indian Child Welfare Act of 1978

Another example of a Petition to the court for the release of all adoption records on file citing the Indian Child Welfare Act. This request was granted and the adoptee received over 50 pages of her adoption records.

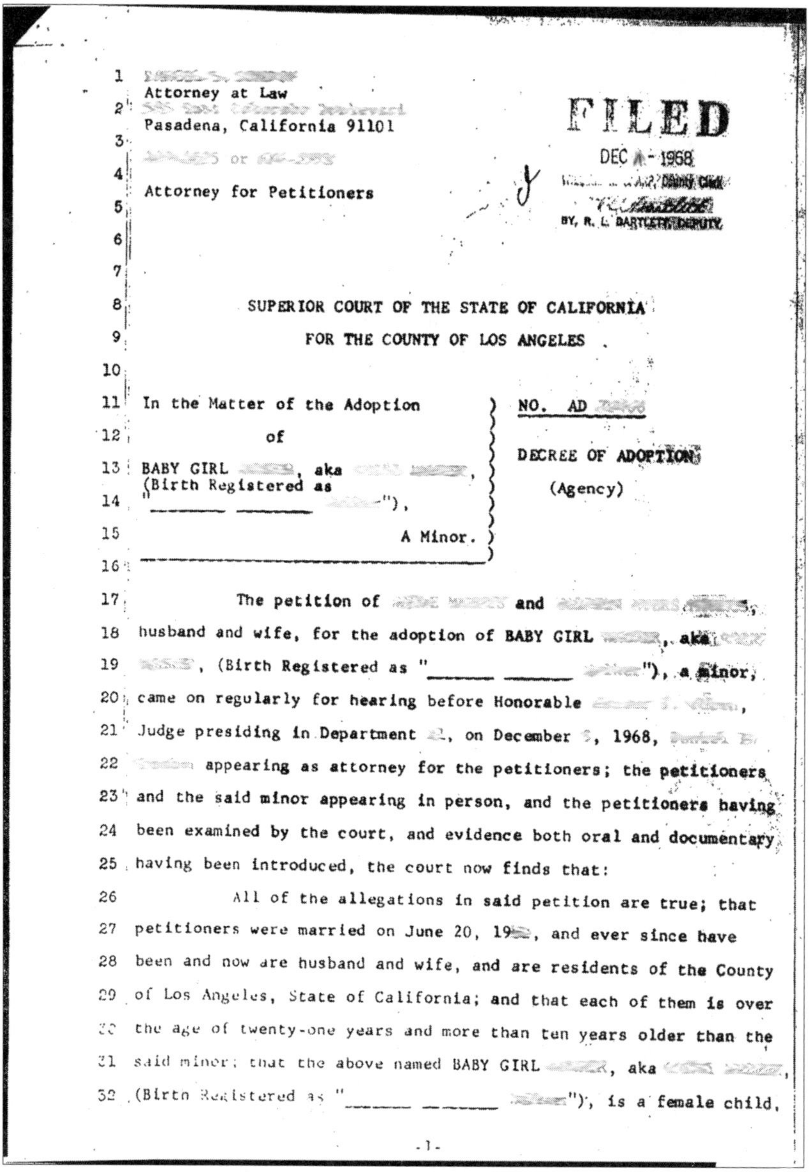

[redacted]
Attorney at Law
[redacted]
Pasadena, California 91101
[redacted] or [redacted]

Attorney for Petitioners

FILED
DEC [redacted] - 1968
[redacted] County Clerk
[redacted]
BY, R. L. BARTLETT, DEPUTY

SUPERIOR COURT OF THE STATE OF CALIFORNIA
FOR THE COUNTY OF LOS ANGELES

In the Matter of the Adoption of BABY GIRL [redacted], aka [redacted], (Birth Registered as "______ ______ [redacted]"), A Minor.	NO. AD [redacted] DECREE OF ADOPTION (Agency)

The petition of [redacted] and [redacted], husband and wife, for the adoption of BABY GIRL [redacted], aka [redacted], (Birth Registered as "______ ______ [redacted]"), a minor, came on regularly for hearing before Honorable [redacted], Judge presiding in Department [redacted], on December [redacted], 1968, [redacted] appearing as attorney for the petitioners; the petitioners and the said minor appearing in person, and the petitioners having been examined by the court, and evidence both oral and documentary having been introduced, the court now finds that:

All of the allegations in said petition are true; that petitioners were married on June 20, 19[redacted], and ever since have been and now are husband and wife, and are residents of the County of Los Angeles, State of California; and that each of them is over the age of twenty-one years and more than ten years older than the said minor; that the above named BABY GIRL [redacted], aka [redacted], (Birth Registered as "______ ______ [redacted]"), is a female child,

-1-

Final Decree of Adoption – Redacted

This is a typical example of a Final Adoption Decree released by the court to an adult adoptee. All identifying information regarding her birth family has been removed by court personnel prior to its release. The courts have different policies and may or may not always provide this document.

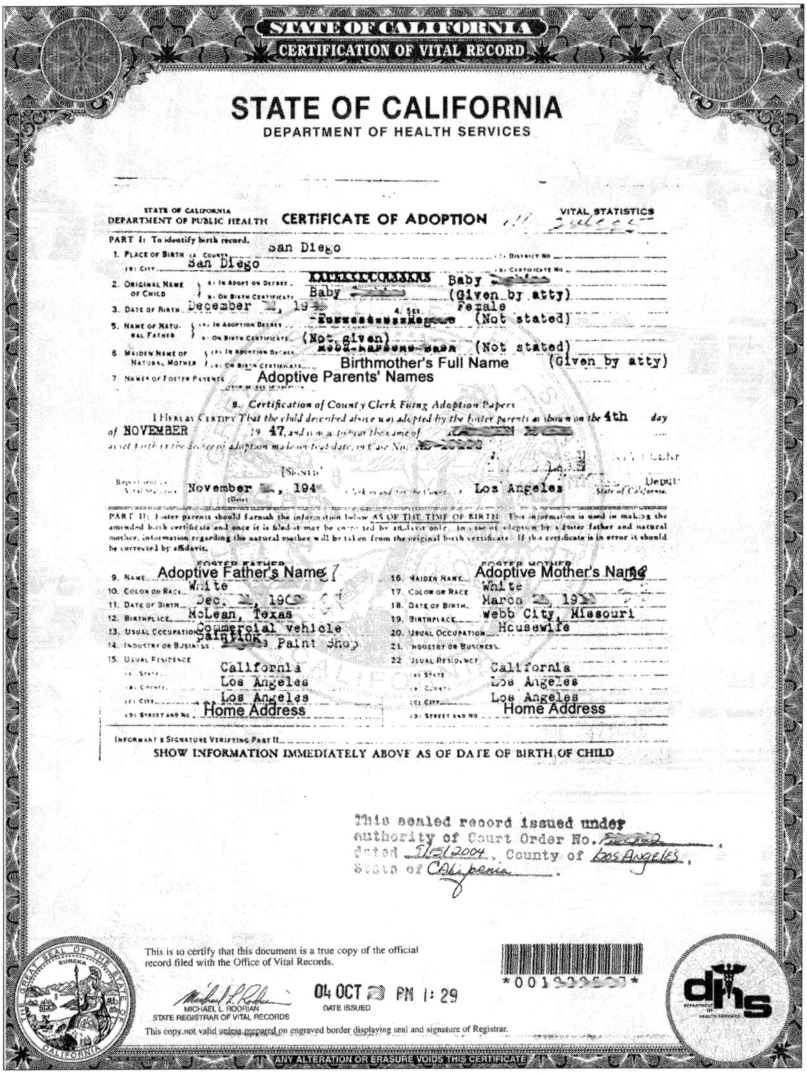

STATE OF CALIFORNIA
CERTIFICATION OF VITAL RECORD

STATE OF CALIFORNIA
DEPARTMENT OF HEALTH SERVICES

STATE OF CALIFORNIA
DEPARTMENT OF PUBLIC HEALTH — CERTIFICATE OF ADOPTION — VITAL STATISTICS

PART I: To identify birth record.

1. Place of Birth (a) County: San Diego — (c) District No.
(b) City: San Diego — (d) Certificate No.
2. Original Name of Child (a) In Adopt on Decree: [redacted] Baby [redacted]
(b) On Birth Certificate: Baby [redacted] (Given by atty)
3. Date of Birth: December [redacted], 19[redacted] — 4. Sex: Female
5. Name of Natural Father (a) In Adoption Decree: [redacted] (Not stated)
(b) On Birth Certificate: (Not given)
6. Maiden Name of Natural Mother (a) In Adoption Decree: [redacted] (Not stated)
(b) On Birth Certificate: Birthmother's Full Name (Given by atty)
7. Names of Foster Parents: Adoptive Parents' Names

8. *Certification of County Clerk Filing Adoption Papers*

I Hereby Certify That the child described above was adopted by the foster parents as shown on the 4th day of NOVEMBER 19 47, and is to bear the name of [redacted] as set forth in the decree of adoption made on that date, in Case No. [redacted]

[Signed]

Reported to Vital Statistics: November [redacted], 194[redacted] (Date) — Clerk in and for the County of Los Angeles, State of California — Deputy

PART II: Foster parents should furnish the information below AS OF THE TIME OF BIRTH. This information is used in making the amended birth certificate and once it is filed it may be corrected by affidavit only. In case of adoption by a foster father and natural mother, information regarding the natural mother will be taken from the original birth certificate. If this certificate is in error it should be corrected by affidavit.

FOSTER FATHER		FOSTER MOTHER	
9. Name	Adoptive Father's Name	16. Maiden Name	Adoptive Mother's Name
10. Color or Race	White	17. Color or Race	White
11. Date of Birth	Dec. [redacted], 19[redacted]	18. Date of Birth	March [redacted], 19[redacted]
12. Birthplace	McLean, Texas	19. Birthplace	Webb City, Missouri
13. Usual Occupation	Commercial vehicle painting	20. Usual Occupation	Housewife
14. Industry or Business	[redacted] Paint Shop	21. Industry or Business	
15. Usual Residence		22. Usual Residence	
(a) State	California	(a) State	California
(b) County	Los Angeles	(b) County	Los Angeles
(c) City	Los Angeles	(c) City	Los Angeles
(d) Street and No.	Home Address	(d) Street and No.	Home Address

Informant's Signature Verifying Part II

SHOW INFORMATION IMMEDIATELY ABOVE AS OF DATE OF BIRTH OF CHILD

This sealed record issued under authority of Court Order No. [redacted] dated 5/5/2004, County of Los Angeles, State of California.

This is to certify that this document is a true copy of the official record filed with the Office of Vital Records.

MICHAEL L. RODRIAN
STATE REGISTRAR OF VITAL RECORDS

04 OCT [redacted] PM 1:29
DATE ISSUED

This copy not valid unless prepared on engraved border displaying seal and signature of Registrar.

ANY ALTERATION OR ERASURE VOIDS THIS CERTIFICATE

Original Certificate of Adoption

This Certificate of Adoption was released to the adoptee by court order. It was originally provided to the Department of Vital Records in order for an Amended Birth Certificate to be filed. It lists the adoptee's original and amended names, and both the birth parents' and the adoptive parents' information. It is extremely rare for an adoptee to ever receive this document, even if they are granted full access to their adoption records.

The Salvation Army Western Territory
Social Services Department - [redacted] Records
[illegible]
[illegible]

[illegible] MATERNITY HOME RECORDS
Authorization for Release

I, ______________________________, authorize The Salvation Army to release to my
☐ birthmother ☐ birthchild ☐ other members of the family ☐ current personal physician
☐ other ______________________________ the following:

☐ Complete Records (Court Order also Required)
☐ Non-identifying medical information (Released to Physician Only)
☐ My name/address/phone number/social security number

This authorization for release is made willingly, knowingly and voluntarily.

Signature: ______________________________

REQUESTER'S CURRENT INFORMATION

Name: ______________________________

Residence Address: ______________________________

Telephone Number (____)______________ Social Security Number: ______________

CASE FILE INFORMATION

Booth Maternity Home: ______________________________
City *State*

Mother's Name at Admittance: ______________________________

Date of Admission: ______________ Child's Date/Time of Birth: ______________

Child's Birth Name: ______________ If no name known, ☐ male? ☐ female?

Other Significant Information: ______________________________

____

****

State of ______________ County of ______________

Subscribed and sworn to before me this ______ day of ______________, 200___. My commission expires
______________.

____
Notary Public

THIS DOCUMENT MUST BE NOTARIZED
Please notify us of a change in address or telephone information

Agency Authorization for Release of Information

Most agencies have their own version of a release form. Triad members may file an authorization to release their information to family members seeking information about them. The form or letter will be placed in the adoption file and the social worker will be alerted if a related Triad member also wants contact. Always ask if there are any consents for contact on file in the agency's record.

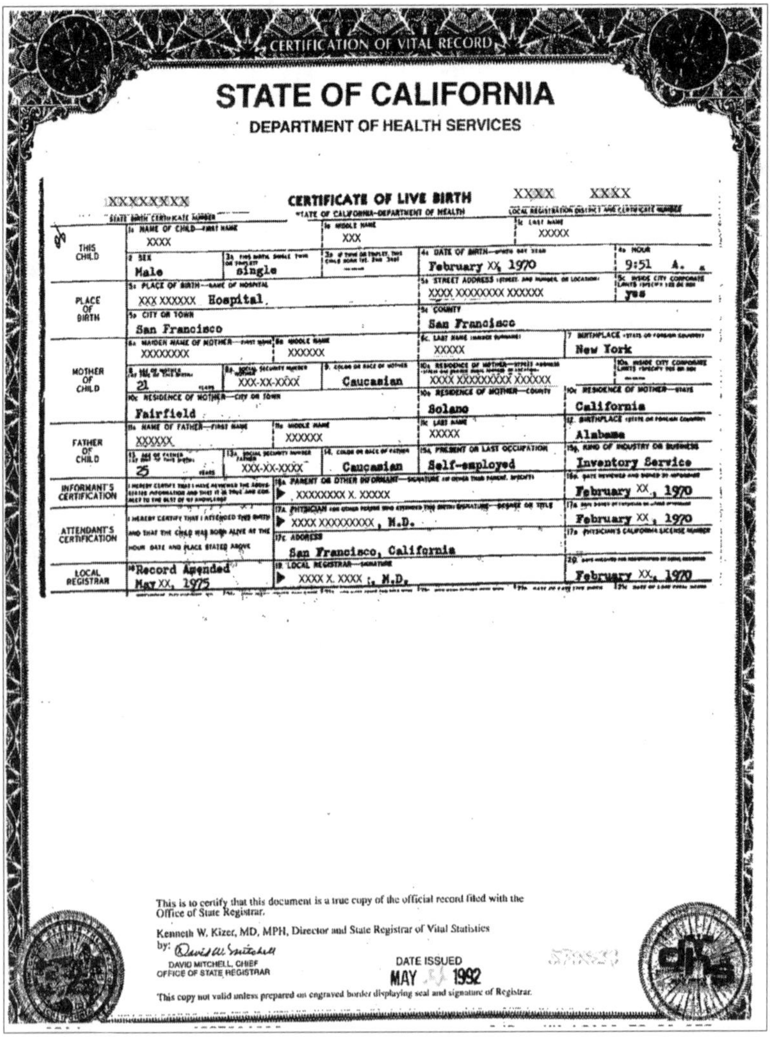

CERTIFICATION OF VITAL RECORD

STATE OF CALIFORNIA

DEPARTMENT OF HEALTH SERVICES

XXXXXXXXX — STATE BIRTH CERTIFICATE NUMBER

CERTIFICATE OF LIVE BIRTH

STATE OF CALIFORNIA—DEPARTMENT OF HEALTH

XXXX XXXX — LOCAL REGISTRATION DISTRICT AND CERTIFICATE NUMBER

THIS CHILD	1a. NAME OF CHILD—FIRST NAME: XXXX	1b. MIDDLE NAME: XXX	1c. LAST NAME: XXXXX	
	2. SEX: Male	3a. SINGLE, TWIN: single	4a. DATE OF BIRTH: February XX, 1970	4b. HOUR: 9:51 A. M.
PLACE OF BIRTH	5a. PLACE OF BIRTH—NAME OF HOSPITAL: XXX XXXXXX Hospital		5b. STREET ADDRESS: XXXX XXXXXXXX XXXXXX	5c. INSIDE CITY CORPORATE LIMITS: yes
	5d. CITY OR TOWN: San Francisco		5e. COUNTY: San Francisco	
MOTHER OF CHILD	6a. MAIDEN NAME OF MOTHER—FIRST NAME: XXXXXXXX	6b. MIDDLE NAME: XXXXXX	6c. LAST NAME: XXXXX	7. BIRTHPLACE: New York
	8. AGE OF MOTHER: 21	8a. SOCIAL SECURITY NUMBER: XXX-XX-XXXX	9. COLOR OR RACE OF MOTHER: Caucasian	10a. RESIDENCE OF MOTHER: XXXX XXXXXXXXX XXXXXX
	10c. RESIDENCE OF MOTHER—CITY OR TOWN: Fairfield		10d. RESIDENCE OF MOTHER—COUNTY: Solano	10e. RESIDENCE OF MOTHER—STATE: California
FATHER OF CHILD	11a. NAME OF FATHER—FIRST NAME: XXXXXX	11b. MIDDLE NAME: XXXXXX	11c. LAST NAME: XXXXX	12. BIRTHPLACE: Alabama
	13. AGE OF FATHER: 25	13a. SOCIAL SECURITY NUMBER: XXX-XX-XXXX	14. COLOR OR RACE OF FATHER: Caucasian	15a. PRESENT OR LAST OCCUPATION: Self-employed; 15b. KIND OF INDUSTRY OR BUSINESS: Inventory Service
INFORMANT'S CERTIFICATION	I hereby certify that I have reviewed the above stated information and that it is true and correct to the best of my knowledge	16a. PARENT OR OTHER INFORMANT—SIGNATURE: XXXXXXXX X. XXXXX		16b. DATE: February XX, 1970
ATTENDANT'S CERTIFICATION	I hereby certify that I attended this birth and that the child was born alive at the hour, date and place stated above	17a. PHYSICIAN: XXXX XXXXXXXXX, M.D.		17b. DATE: February XX, 1970
		17c. ADDRESS: San Francisco, California		17d. PHYSICIAN'S CALIFORNIA LICENSE NUMBER
LOCAL REGISTRAR	*Record Amended May XX, 1975	18. LOCAL REGISTRAR—SIGNATURE: XXXX X. XXXX, M.D.		19. DATE: February XX, 1970

This is to certify that this document is a true copy of the official record filed with the Office of State Registrar.

Kenneth W. Kizer, MD, MPH, Director and State Registrar of Vital Statistics

by: David W. Mitchell

DAVID MITCHELL, CHIEF OFFICE OF STATE REGISTRAR

DATE ISSUED MAY XX 1992

This copy not valid unless prepared on engraved border displaying seal and signature of Registrar.

Amended Birth Certificate

When an Amended Birth Certificate is issued, it replaces the Original Birth Certificate, which is then "sealed" and cannot be opened without a court order. The amended certificate appears as if the adoptee was born to the adopting parents. This certificate denotes the date in which "Record Amended." Other certificates may use the phrase "Date Issued" or "Date Recorded." The date, which is usually six months or more from the date of birth, can provide a clue as to when the adoption was finalized. This can be helpful in a search if the adoption date is unknown. The State Birth Certificate Number and County Registrar Number will be the same as on the Original Birth Certificate in many states, but not all.

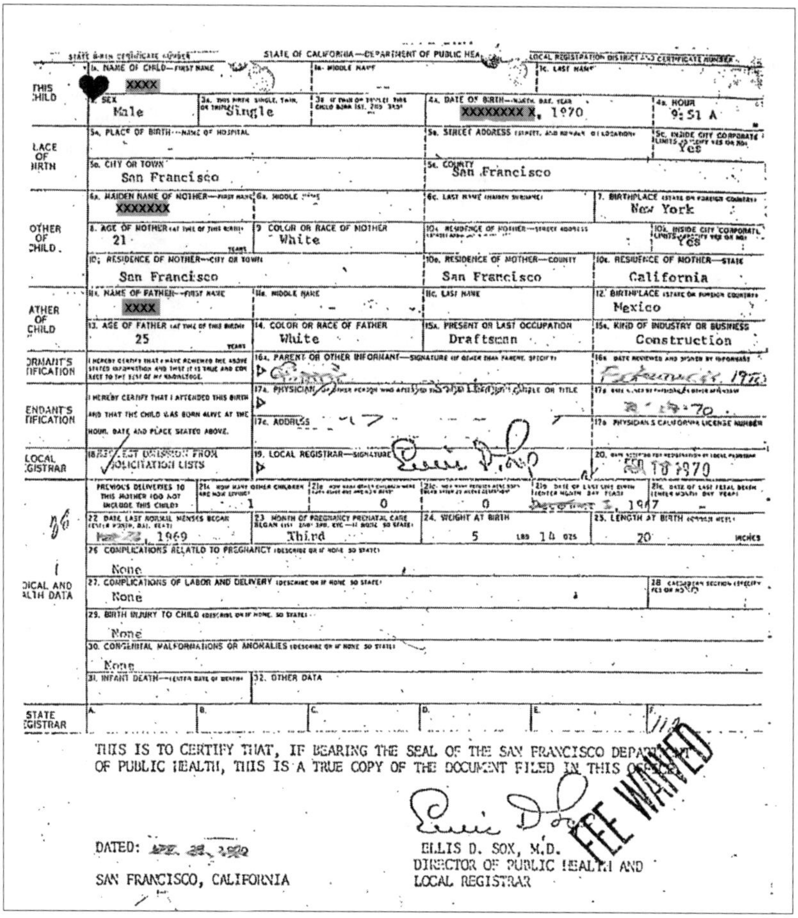

STATE BIRTH CERTIFICATE NUMBER — STATE OF CALIFORNIA—DEPARTMENT OF PUBLIC HEALTH — LOCAL REGISTRATION DISTRICT AND CERTIFICATE NUMBER

THIS CHILD
[redacted]
1a. NAME OF CHILD—FIRST NAME: XXXX
1b. MIDDLE NAME
1c. LAST NAME
2. SEX: Male
3a. THIS BIRTH SINGLE, TWIN, OR TRIPLET: Single
3b. IF TWIN OR TRIPLET, THIS CHILD BORN 1ST, 2ND, 3RD
4a. DATE OF BIRTH—MONTH, DAY, YEAR: XXXXXXXX X, 1970
4b. HOUR: 9:51 A

PLACE OF BIRTH
5a. PLACE OF BIRTH—NAME OF HOSPITAL
5b. STREET ADDRESS
5c. INSIDE CITY CORPORATE LIMITS: Yes
5d. CITY OR TOWN: San Francisco
5e. COUNTY: San Francisco

MOTHER OF CHILD
6a. MAIDEN NAME OF MOTHER—FIRST NAME: XXXXXXX
6b. MIDDLE NAME
6c. LAST NAME (MAIDEN SURNAME)
7. BIRTHPLACE (STATE OR FOREIGN COUNTRY): New York
8. AGE OF MOTHER (AT TIME OF THIS BIRTH): 21 YEARS
9. COLOR OR RACE OF MOTHER: White
10a. RESIDENCE OF MOTHER—STREET ADDRESS
10b. INSIDE CITY CORPORATE LIMITS: Yes
10c. RESIDENCE OF MOTHER—CITY OR TOWN: San Francisco
10d. RESIDENCE OF MOTHER—COUNTY: San Francisco
10e. RESIDENCE OF MOTHER—STATE: California

FATHER OF CHILD
11a. NAME OF FATHER—FIRST NAME: XXXX
11b. MIDDLE NAME
11c. LAST NAME
12. BIRTHPLACE (STATE OR FOREIGN COUNTRY): Mexico
13. AGE OF FATHER (AT TIME OF THIS BIRTH): 25 YEARS
14. COLOR OR RACE OF FATHER: White
15a. PRESENT OR LAST OCCUPATION: Draftsman
15b. KIND OF INDUSTRY OR BUSINESS: Construction

INFORMANT'S CERTIFICATION
I HEREBY CERTIFY THAT I HAVE REVIEWED THE ABOVE STATED INFORMATION AND THAT IT IS TRUE AND CORRECT TO THE BEST OF MY KNOWLEDGE.
16a. PARENT OR OTHER INFORMANT—SIGNATURE
16b. DATE REVIEWED AND SIGNED BY INFORMANT: February, 1970

ATTENDANT'S CERTIFICATION
I HEREBY CERTIFY THAT I ATTENDED THIS BIRTH AND THAT THE CHILD WAS BORN ALIVE AT THE HOUR, DATE AND PLACE STATED ABOVE.
17a. PHYSICIAN OR OTHER PERSON WHO ATTENDED—SIGNATURE AND DEGREE OR TITLE
17b. DATE SIGNED BY PHYSICIAN: 2-19-70
17c. ADDRESS
17d. PHYSICIAN'S CALIFORNIA LICENSE NUMBER

LOCAL REGISTRAR
18. REQUEST DELETION FROM SOLICITATION LISTS
19. LOCAL REGISTRAR—SIGNATURE
20. DATE ACCEPTED FOR REGISTRATION BY LOCAL REGISTRAR: FEB 18 1970

MEDICAL AND HEALTH DATA
PREVIOUS DELIVERIES TO THIS MOTHER (DO NOT INCLUDE THIS CHILD)
21a. HOW MANY OTHER CHILDREN ARE NOW LIVING: 1
21b. HOW MANY OTHER CHILDREN WERE BORN ALIVE BUT ARE NOW DEAD: 0
21c. HOW MANY FETUSES WERE BORN DEAD: 0
21d. DATE OF LAST LIVE BIRTH: December 1, 1967
21e. DATE OF LAST FETAL DEATH
22. DATE LAST NORMAL MENSES BEGAN: 1969
23. MONTH OF PREGNANCY PRENATAL CARE BEGAN: Third
24. WEIGHT AT BIRTH: 5 LBS 14 OZS
25. LENGTH AT BIRTH: 20 INCHES
26. COMPLICATIONS RELATED TO PREGNANCY (DESCRIBE OR IF NONE SO STATE): None
27. COMPLICATIONS OF LABOR AND DELIVERY (DESCRIBE OR IF NONE SO STATE): None
28. CAESAREAN SECTION (SPECIFY YES OR NO): No
29. BIRTH INJURY TO CHILD (DESCRIBE OR IF NONE, SO STATE): None
30. CONGENITAL MALFORMATIONS OR ANOMALIES (DESCRIBE OR IF NONE SO STATE): None
31. INFANT DEATH—ENTER DATE OF DEATH
32. OTHER DATA

STATE REGISTRAR: A. B. C. D. E. F.

THIS IS TO CERTIFY THAT, IF BEARING THE SEAL OF THE SAN FRANCISCO DEPARTMENT OF PUBLIC HEALTH, THIS IS A TRUE COPY OF THE DOCUMENT FILED IN THIS OFFICE.

FEE WAIVED

DATED: APR. 28, 1980
SAN FRANCISCO, CALIFORNIA

ELLIS D. SOX, M.D.
DIRECTOR OF PUBLIC HEALTH AND LOCAL REGISTRAR

Original Birth Certificate

The *Original Birth Certificate* is issued with the baby's name at birth, plus the birth parents' personal information. It stays in place until an adoption is finalized and is then replaced by the *Amended Birth Certificate.* The original certificate is then referred to as "sealed." Many times, it is just that – sealed in an envelope and kept on file with the amended certificate. In California, the certificate numbers on the original and amended birth certificates are always the same.

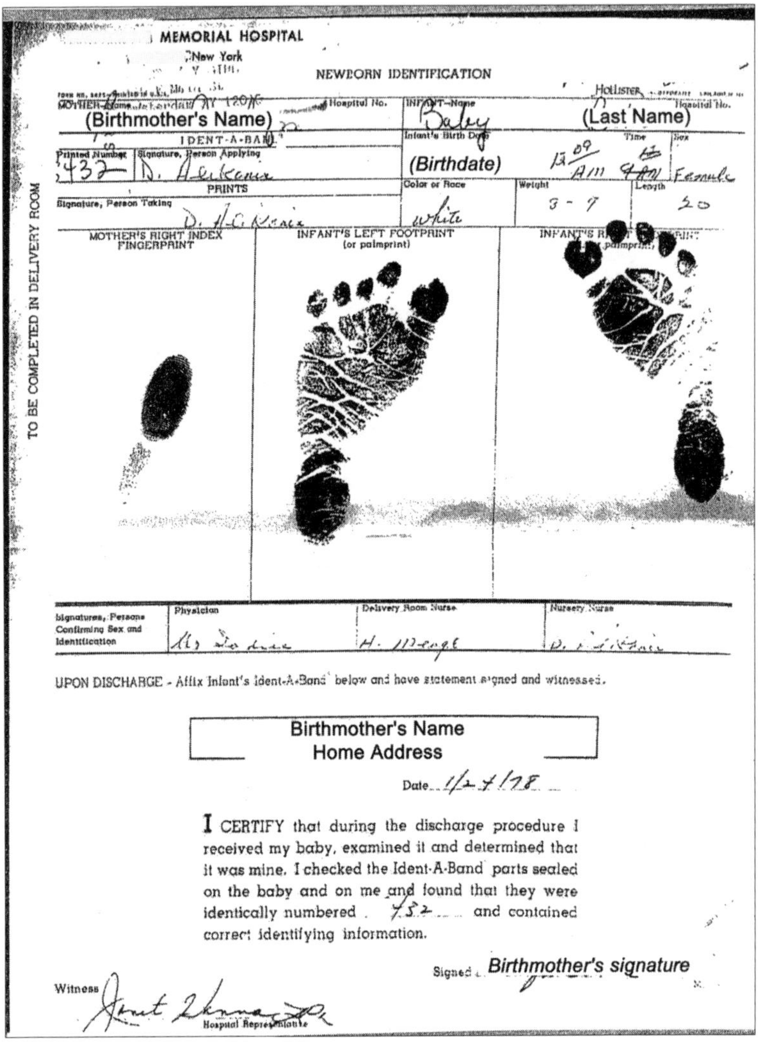

MEMORIAL HOSPITAL
New York

NEWBORN IDENTIFICATION

TO BE COMPLETED IN DELIVERY ROOM

MOTHER—Name (Birthmother's Name)	Hospital No.	INFANT—Name Baby (Last Name)		Hospital No.
IDENT-A-BAND		Infant's Birth Date (Birthdate)	Time	Sex Female
Printed Number 432	Signature, Person Applying D. [illegible]	Color or Race white	Weight 3 - 7	Length 20
PRINTS				
Signature, Person Taking D. [illegible]				

MOTHER'S RIGHT INDEX FINGERPRINT

INFANT'S LEFT FOOTPRINT (or palmprint)

INFANT'S RIGHT FOOTPRINT (or palmprint)

Signatures, Persons Confirming Sex and Identification	Physician	Delivery Room Nurse	Nursery Nurse
	[illegible]	H. [illegible]	D. [illegible]

UPON DISCHARGE - Affix Infant's Ident-A-Band below and have statement signed and witnessed.

Birthmother's Name
Home Address

Date 1/27/78

I CERTIFY that during the discharge procedure I received my baby, examined it and determined that it was mine. I checked the Ident-A-Band parts sealed on the baby and on me and found that they were identically numbered 432 and contained correct identifying information.

Signed Birthmother's signature

Witness [illegible]
Hospital Representative

Hospital Record (Partial)

Some hospital destroy their records after time, others keep them indefinitely. This example is a portion of what Cara received when she requested her records from the hospital. (See *Cara's Story: A Sense of Self*). Many times hospital records will be sent to an adoptee heavily redacted as it is noted in those records that the baby is being placed for adoption. In Cara's case, no such notes existed as her birth mother had no intention of placing Cara for adoption at that time.

NEW YORK STATE DEPARTMENT OF HEALTH ADOPTION INFORMATION REGISTRY

NON-IDENTIFYING INFORMATION REPORT

Registrant's Name: Adoptee's Full Name

Registry # xxx-xxxxxxxx

Non-identifying Information: Concerning the birth parents at the time of the adoptee's birth.

ITEM	Mother	Father
Age	21	22
Heritage:		
Nationality	USA	Poland
Ethnic Background	Not reported	Not reported
Race	White	White
Physical Appearance:	Not reported	Not reported
Height	" "	" "
Weight	" "	" "
Hair Color	" "	" "
Eye Color	" "	" "
Skin Color	" "	" "
Other Characteristics	Not reported	Not reported
Religion	Jewish	Jewish
Education	Not reported	Not reported
Occupation	" "	" "
Talents, Hobbies And Interests	Student	Housewife

Health History of Birth Mother: Your mother was an epileptic. She had several seizures during the pregnancy. You were born at 7 months and weighed less than 5 pounds when bought home.

Health History of Birth Father: No information was provided.

Facts and circumstances relating to the nature and cause of the adoption: Your father married your mother. Your mother felt incapable of caring for a child because of her epilepsy and friction between herself and your father. They placed you for adoption. The adoption was handled through a private placement. An agency was not involved in the adoption.

This report was completed by: Peter M. Carucci, Director

Non Identifying Background Information (New York State Information)

Non-Identifying Information provided by agencies or courts are usually informative, full of medical, and social history. Other reports are scant, giving as little information as possible, and are sometimes also inaccurate. This is an example of the information provided to an adoptee who requested this information from the State of New York's Department of Health. The birthfather's information listed "housewife for his "Talents, Hobbies & Interests". When the adoptee wrote to ask for clarification as to whether *all* of the information was reversed for the father and mother, she waited six months for their response; that it was only that particular information that was inaccurately reported. Clearly, little care was taken in preparing this report, as even "Student" and "Housewife" should have fallen under "Occupation." Even the physical appearances are listed among the many things "Not Reported." Sadly, this report is fairly standard fare for those who were born and adopted in New York and were not placed through private agencies.

BACKGROUND INFORMATION:

BIRTHMOTHER:

She was born in 1927 in Oklahoma. Her parents were divorced,when she was young and she never saw her father again. Although,she knew that he resided in Texas.She was raised by her mother and stepfather. She stated that she had one brother,but he was deceased. Her mother later lived in Kansas.

She was attractive with a fair complexion,blond wavy hair and bright blue eyes. She was slender. Her education was unknown. Her religion was protestant.

She was married twice. She divorced her first husband in 1946 and separated from her second husband in 1949. She had one son born in Colorado and she stated that he was well taken care of,but did not disclose his whereabouts.

She worked as a cook and a waitress. However,since 1946 she worked as a prostitute. She had a police record in Colorado for using narcotics. She reported that she used morphine,not heroin.

She died in 1956 in Wyoming. She was found frozen to death by the side of the highway. Autopsy revealed that she was under the influence of narcotics. They thought that her car stalled and she tried to walk for help. She lay down beside the road and froze to death. She had left another son born on [illegible] in 1953. He had an adoptive home in Wyoming.

BIRTHFATHER:

His identity is unknown according to the birthmother.

CIRCUMSTANCES:

When the birthmother entered the hospital to have her daughter,she requested adoption services. She stated that she coudn't provide a home for her child. However,before signing relinquishment documents she disappeared. She turned up later in Wyoming,where she had deceased on [illegible],1956.

Non Identifying Background Information (Agency Information)

This example is part of over 20 pages of non identifying information provided to Lorraine's request by the agency (see *Lorraine's Search: An Angel in the Snow*). Some of the information was re-typed, leaving out identifying information, but yet she also received intact copies of the notes from her birthmother's interviews with nothing taken out. No two people ever get the same kind of non identifying information. We regularly see dramatic differences in the type of information received from the same agency providing reports to two different people requesting records at the same time.

CHAPTER 9

Lorraine's Search

An Angel in the Snow

When Lorraine contacted us, her expectations were remarkably modest compared with other clients. From the Non-Identifying Information provided by the adoption agency, Lorraine was already equipped with the knowledge that her birthmother had lived a hard life and died a terrible death. Lorraine simply wanted to know her birthmother's real name, where she was buried, and the circumstances of her death. We were determined to do what we could for her.

Lorraine was 42 years of age when she came to us upon the referral of Kristen's childhood friend. A pretty woman, with a head full of blond curls, she was married with small children and living in Eureka, California. The information Lorraine gave us came directly from the county adoption agency in San Francisco that had placed her with a foster family soon after her birth in the early 1950s. This information was rather general, as it often is with adoption agencies. In our many years of investigative work, we've seen how agencies hold back facts, making decisions about what to record and what not to divulge in order to protect the identity, privacy and even the feelings of the individuals involved, be it the birthparents or the adoptees. Thankfully, this agency didn't hold back anything—they told it like it was.

Here are the two short paragraphs in the agency's report that we had to go on:

> Birthmother was slender and attractive with bright blue eyes, wavy blond hair and a fair complexion. She worked as a cook and waitress. However, since 1946 she had worked as a prostitute. She had a police record in Nevada for using narcotics. She reported that she used morphine, not heroin.
>
> She died in 1956 in Wyoming. She was found frozen to death by the side of the highway. Autopsy revealed that she was under the influence of narcotics. They thought that her car stalled and she tried to walk for help. She lay down beside the road and froze to death. She left an adopted son born in 1953 who lived with his adoptive family in Wyoming.

In the Name of a Mother

We began the search in 1997. We were looking for a nameless woman that had died in 1956, somewhere in Wyoming. Our first task was to determine if there were any old records regarding a lady that froze to death in Wyoming in this time period. We felt that when we found this information, we would know Lorraine's birthmother's name, and where she had lived, worked, and died. We started out looking for news articles in Wyoming for 1956 that might have reported such a death. During our initial discussions, we had a slight edge because Ava had once lived in the San Francisco Bay area in the 1950's. She remembered that the newspapers often published articles about the prostitutes who would travel and work between San Francisco, Reno and Cheyenne, Wyoming. We got out a map of the U.S and began studying the towns, roads and highways between and within the three states. Ava intuitively picked a central point along the route, and we thought it was as good a starting point as any.

Judy called the local librarian in this Wyoming town and asked if she would check the old 1956 newspapers to see if anything was written about a woman who had been found in the area frozen to death by the side of the road. This librarian turned out to be helpful and diligent way beyond the call of duty—she actually remembered such an incident happening when she was a child in the mid 1950's!

The librarian started us off by locating all the news articles she could find on the tragedy—and the actual date and facts of the incident confirmed that we had, indeed, found the right town. This wonderful woman was relentless. She kept digging away, calling us every time she found more information.

It needs to be noted that that there are scads of towns along the highways in Wyoming. The fact that Ava put her finger on the exact spot on the map was sheer luck!

While the librarian was busy muddling through stacks of old newspaper articles, Judy called the town coroner to obtain a copy of the office's record of the death. We wanted to find out where she'd been buried and who had paid for her burial. We were pretty puzzled when the coroner's office told Judy they couldn't help us because all the records between 1950 and 1960 had been destroyed. That sounded strange to us. Were they simply being too lazy to go dig through old records? Was it because Lorraine's mother had been a prostitute, living on the edge of society? Or was it remotely possible that there was some greater degree of foul play involved?

The next move was to call the Sheriff's office to see whether they had any records on this incident. They were much more helpful than the coroner. The deputy we spoke with pulled up the old files of the woman who had frozen to death outside of town, and was very surprised when we told her that the Coroner's records for that date had been destroyed. Shortly after speaking with the sheriff's office, we received a call from the coroner's office and they admitted that they did in fact locate the records of the woman who had died out in the snow. Had the Sheriff and the coroner had a few discussions in the meantime? Maybe her death wasn't as innocent as portrayed in the papers after all. See what you think after reading the following paragraphs.

Angel in the Snow

According to newspaper accounts of 1956, Lorraine's birthmother, who was known as 'Tiffany Hart,' was reported to be 23 when she froze to death in the winter snow of Wyoming. She was found on her back in a spread-eagled position, frozen hard and with her mouth wide open. Initial information released by the Sheriff's department gave the following sequence of events that led up to 'Miss Hart's' death:

> At 6 a.m. on a February Sunday morning, Miss Hart left (town omitted) to allegedly find a friend of hers who was working as a herder of sheep in a section of the Red Desert. She was accompanied by a man she had hired to do the driving, Jim Davis, who drove the vehicle, a 1956 Oldsmobile 88 that was later found bogged down in a gully drifted over by snow.

By Jim Davis' account, the car broke down and 'Miss Hart' *decided* to leave the car around 3:00 p.m. on Sunday in a snowstorm to see if she could get help. He stayed in the car to wait for her return. He reported that he remained in the car all night, and honked the horn and flashed the car lights every now and then in the hope that she would find her way back. It was not until around 9:00 a.m. Monday morning that Jim Davis left the car. He thinks he wandered about 10 miles before coming across the Red Rock sheep camp. Jim Davis was then taken to Tucker Mays' service station by a Red Rock truck driver. They notified the Sheriff's department that a woman was lost in the Red Desert.

A search party, which included Tucker Mays and Jim Davis, set out to retrace Mr. Davis' steps to the Oldsmobile. Mays reported that Jim Davis was foot sore and disoriented, and had a lot of trouble leading them back to the vehicle.

The sheriff's office then organized a rescue operation to begin at 4:00 a.m. on Tuesday. Ten men were on standby alert. In spite of the cold weather and icy, piercing wind, at approximately 8:30 a.m. the body was found by two local men, Red Smith and Leroy Edwards, who had volunteered to help search. By this time, 'Tiffany Hart' had been missing and without shelter in the freezing weather since 3:00 p.m. Sunday afternoon—over 40 hours. She had fallen or lain in the snow on a ridge about 1.1 miles from the car. She was described as having bleached blond hair and weighing about 130 pounds. She was wearing a brown knit sweater, gabardine slacks, and full-length beige coat, head scarf, and a pair of low heeled oxfords. Though found early on Tuesday morning, the authorities had to wait a whole day for her body to thaw out enough for them to be able to take fingerprints.

The Autopsy

Once her body had thawed, it was clear to see that 'Tiffany Hart' had lost her way, stumbling, wandering and falling again and again in the snow. Her hands and ankles were covered with sagebrush cuts. It looked like she had finally dropped to the ground and been unable to get back on her feet. The autopsy also revealed that at the time of her death, she had been under the influence of narcotics.

Our helpful librarian put us in touch with people who'd been part of the search for the body and others who had known Lorraine's birthmother. We don't mind admitting that good, caring people are the best allies we've ever had in our line of work. Their personal contacts and their own viewpoints on events turn up some of the most priceless information. In a small town like this one, our angel of a librarian was able to guide us through the research that would have really slowed our search process down if we were doing it on our own.

We were so relieved the day the librarian called to say she'd found the obituary that confirmed Lorraine's birthmother's real name. It was published the same week as the body of 'Tiffany Hart' was found. The wording was short and sweet. It was clear from the facts that when she died, she was actually a few years older than she appeared to those who initially found her in the snow:

> Private funeral services for Clara Marie Roberts, 28 will be held at 2 p.m. Wednesday, at the Henderson funeral home, the Rev. Richard Garrison officiating. The body of Miss Roberts was found Tuesday on the Red Desert. An autopsy revealed she died of exposure and freezing. Miss Roberts was born July 8, 1927, in Enid, Oklahoma. She was a resident of (town name omitted) for eight months. The only survivor listed is Miss Roberts' mother, Mrs. Stella Sizemore, now residing in Kentucky. Burial will be in Mountain View cemetery.

The True Picture of Ms. Clara Roberts

During the year that it took us to clear up the truth about Clara Roberts we continued to send information to Lorraine as we found it. It was important to us that the whole picture came out from the scattered facts and tidbits we were acquiring week by week, month by month. After all, these were people's lives we were dealing with. Lorraine would never get to meet her birthmother, but we wanted her to at least have the truth about her life and death.

Personal interviews with the key participants at the time of Clara Roberts' death helped everything fall into place. Through our librarian in the small town, we got in touch with Mr. Edwards, the herder who had found her body over 40 years ago. Although now quite elderly, he remembered the incident clearly. He told us that when he'd found her she looked like an angel in the snow, which made him suspicious. Mr. Edwards said:

> "When you freeze to death, you're all balled up. You're not spread eagle."

Another kind woman who called us said that although she was a little girl at the time, she remembered hearing people talk about how the accounts in the newspaper had protected Jim Davis. He was reported to be a 'friend' to Clara but in reality, the local lady told us, he was a known pimp, and went on to say:

> "That son of a bitch. He killed her. Had her out there to service all the herders, looks like they had car trouble and he made her go for help."

Interestingly enough, we learned that Jim Davis' stepfather was a city policeman—Ray Parks. And Davis' half-brother, Mike Parks, turned out to be the coroner who had given us the run around. So that's small town politics for you.

Before these rather sordid family connections came to light, the three of us had been wondering if maybe Clara hadn't overdosed out in the snow, or maybe just worn herself out by being on the drugs and wandering around in those impossible conditions to the point that she just couldn't go on. By now we had the clear impression that she probably was forced out of the car into the winter wind and snow by her pimp.

It seems clear that Clara was on her way to provide her services at the Red Rock sheep camp. Along the way, something went very wrong and she lost her life. It's equally clear, that whether foul play was involved or not, no one was looking out for Clara Roberts and she was probably in no condition to do so for herself. She was alone and she didn't survive.

The coroner report, which took us so much effort to finally obtain, gave us a lot of the information we needed to complete the story of Clara Roberts' death and burial. We now had the name of the lady who'd paid for her funeral—it was Twila Harper who had been the town's Madam. In the report, she confirmed that 'Tiffany Hart' had been Clara's alias while she worked. In addition to these facts, we now knew where Clara's grave was.

An Understanding Daughter

When all the facts were finally on the table, we all cried. It was so sad. We hate bringing bad news to a client. But we knew Lorraine needed to hear her birthmother's story.

Lorraine was very sympathetic to her mother. We emphasized to her how young Clara had been when she'd relinquished Lorraine. Times were bad then and she had been so alone. Clara's own parents had divorced when she was very young, and Clara never even knew her father and was raised by her mother and stepfather, who moved around from town to town. With no one to turn to for help or guidance, Clara turned to drugs and eventually prostitution.

We reassured Lorraine that at the very least her birthmother had made sure to get her a decent home. She'd had enough presence of mind to go through with her pregnancy and make sure that her daughter was placed somewhere safe. We knew that Clara had also placed a son for adoption in 1953. We were willing to find him for Lorraine to connect with, but in addition to illness in her family, Lorraine felt that her journey thus far had been too emotionally exhausting and decided to put any further search efforts for her brother on hold indefinitely. We felt satisfied that we were at least able to provide Lorraine with her birthmother's name, where she was buried and some answers about the details of her life and death.

We have never forgotten the tragic story of that young angel in the snow and hope someday to be able to visit the cemetery where she is buried and place flowers on her grave.

CHAPTER 10

Jon' s Search

You Only Get One Life

Every so often a case comes along that tries everybody's patience. Nothing seems to pan out as it should, and month-by-month the frustration level goes up. A client may start to question our abilities and we in turn become more and more frustrated. But the way we look at it is, the more we've put into a case, the more we want to solve it. That was Jon's story in a nutshell.

Jon was born in 1970 and relinquished for adoption. Most of our clients are well adjusted and easy to work with -- Jon wasn't one of those clients. He experienced extreme mood swings and later told us that he'd abused drugs for many years. In his mind, he'd always believed reconnecting with his birth family would somehow solve his problems. In 1998, at age 28, he finally decided to find out if this was really the case.

Jon was living in Southern California when he contacted us to locate his birthmother. During an initial conversation, he mentioned his motivation for reconnecting with his birth family: *"I just have to know—you only get one life."* We couldn't argue with that.

We started out by contacting the agency that had arranged Jon's adoption. They sent us on a wild-goose chase that ended up delaying Jon's search for four long years. This nationwide adoption agency is notorious for dishing out inaccurate information. Sometimes, the 'facts' they present are just flat out wrong. It's not clear whether this is a deliberate practice to deter search efforts, or just plain careless work on their part. Whatever the reason, it made our job much, much harder.

This agency gave us Jon's birthmother's maiden name as 'Shields,' her age seventeen, and her birthplace California. She was reported to have a younger sister at the time, aged six. The nine-year age difference between them stood out as unusual. Tracking down Jon's birthfather would be useless, the record suggested, because he knew nothing of the birth or of the adoption.

We had to locate all the female Shields born in California who were seventeen years of age in 1970, with a little sister nine years younger. Because we didn't find a Shields girl with a sister nine years younger, we assumed the sister information might be incorrect and began searching based on the birthmother's information alone.

What a chore it was—tracking each one of the Shields women down through their lives, the various marriages they'd had, and places they had lived, and so forth—right up to the last stage where we finally had the correct phone numbers and were ready to call them up. In all, we contacted 120 women and it took us three years to do it, because in addition to the main investigation, we were performing 120 separate investigations of each of these women, just to make sure Jon's birthmother wasn't missed. We'd find one, be sure it was her, get so excited and then discover it was just a false alarm. By a strange coincidence, one of Judy's old high school classmates turned up on our list. The woman acted so strangely when we contacted her, (without revealing that Judy knew her from school) that we suspected she was hiding something. We followed up only to realize that the reason she was acting oddly was simply because she was drunk every time we spoke.

But the final result of the 120 Shields women we investigated—*Jon's birthmother wasn't among them.*

This was an extremely frustrating time for everyone involved. We couldn't believe how slowly the search was going, and neither could Jon. In fact, he frequently became angry and rude with us, making it even more difficult for us to have the heart to keep going. He'd threaten to fire us, which frankly we wouldn't have minded all that much. But then, he'd call back and beg us not to quit on him, and of course, all would be forgiven. In spite of his mood swings, we really liked Jon and understood his frustration, since we were feeling it on our end as well.

Jon's father wasn't making things any easier. He made no secret of his feeling that we weren't doing the job right, and that he could do it better himself. His questions about our abilities put doubt in Jon's mind over and over again. This was a pressure that added to Jon's already fragile emotional state. The longer we went without finding his birthmother, the more upset he became. We also knew Jon had a somewhat strained relationship with his mother during this period, she just wasn't happy about him searching for his birthmother. Jon wasn't getting any support or encouragement from anyone but us.

The one thing we and Jon agreed on was that we didn't want to quit. We'd never failed to solve a case involving a California adoption and weren't about to now. Though we fired him a couple of times and he fired us once, Jon became like a little brother to us. Today we're so glad we kept going together.

Working all the Angles

Jon's record stated that he was part Cherokee. To give an idea of how desperate we were for a break in the case, we even attempted to unseal his birth information under the Federal Indian Child Welfare act of 1978. But the court wouldn't release anything because we didn't have the documents to prove that he was Cherokee, even though it was stated in his NIDI! That's the vicious circle we were trying to break out of.

The trail had gone cold and we knew that something was very wrong about the information we'd been given. *But which bit of Jon's Non-Identifying Information was wrong?* Kristen started thinking that maybe Jon's birthmother had come from another state and gone to a maternity home in California. We knew that the particular adoption agency that was involved in Jon's adoption and supplied the NIDI often used a home run by the Salvation Army, though the agency would never voluntarily reveal that to an adoptee. We figured it was worth a shot. At this point, we had nothing to lose; the search was at a standstill.

We called the Salvation Army and landed a friendly person. We gave this helpful lady Jon's birth name, 'Jimmy Shields' and his date of birth. Things went silent while she typed the information into her computer. We were holding our breath, when she excitedly said, "Have him call me!"

We all got the chills and knew right away that this was our breakthrough. This helpful woman knew something, but could only reveal it to Jon. We were so excited to call Jon with some good news for a change. We contacted Jon and he called the Salvation Army lady straight away. He called us back with the best possible news—he had verification that his birthmother had indeed stayed at their maternity home, and they had his birth and adoption information still on file! The home quickly released Non-Identifying Information to him as soon as he provided the required proof of identity. As we had come to suspect, the adoption agency had reported the wrong information about where Jon' birthmother was born! It wasn't California at all; she was born in Kentucky.

This wonderful Salvation Army lady also provided Jon with more NIDI than he had received from the agency, for which we were all extremely grateful. Among other things, we found out that Jon's birthfather had been a football player and his birthmother a cheerleader. More significantly, we discovered that Jon was given a birth name—Jimmy Allen Michellin. This new surname gave us Jon's birthfather's last name!

We checked the Kentucky birth register for a Shields female—and were relieved to find that there was just a handful born in this state. You can imagine the thrill when we found the one who fit the description that the original agency had given us. In 1970, she was the right age (17), and her sister was also the right age (6). They'd both been born in the same county in Kentucky, a long, long way from California.

Focus on the Father

This Shield's woman's first name was Stacey. She'd been married five or six times, changing her name as she went, and we didn't feel like tracking her for another four years. And so we turned our attention to Jon's birthfather, now that we knew his last name and that he was also born in Kentucky. We had a feeling he'd be our short cut to solving this case.

His last name was an unusual one—Michellin. His first name was whited out on the NIDI, all we could make out was that it was five letters long, and had an 'e' and 'y' in the name. We used the Kentucky birth index to locate all the Michellin boys who were 17 years of age in 1970. There was only one with a first name that fit with the `e' and the `y'—Leroy Michellin. And—he was born in the same county as Stacey! It was an amazing moment. After four long years of searching, we'd cracked the case in one day, simply by having accurate information to work with.

Once we'd located Leroy, Kristen got on the phone with him and proceeded with her usual cautious manner. He had an open, friendly way about him and when Kristen asked him several innocuous questions about his life, he happily answered them. When his answers corresponded to the NIDI we had, Kristen was satisfied that he was indeed Jon's birthfather. Even though Kristen maintained a calm, professional manner on the telephone, she, Ava and Judy were jumping up and down, arms in the air, at this final victory for Jon's search!

Kristen told Leroy he might want to sit down, that she had something important to tell him—it was time to get down to the nitty-gritty. Kristen said that she knew he had dated a girl named Shields back in 1970. She didn't say `Stacey' because she was hoping he'd give away her first name to further confirm that we had earlier identified the right person. He admitted that he had dated a *Stacey* Shields in his senior year. At this point, Kristen gently told him that we helped adopted people find their birth families...Leroy quickly interrupted her, happily blurting out:

> "You must be calling about Jimmy!"

Kristen nearly fell out of her chair! According to the adoption agency, this man wasn't supposed to know anything about being a father to a baby born in California. Turned out, he knew everything. "*I love him already,*" Leroy said, and went on to agree to full contact. Leroy also helped fill in some of the blanks in the story. According to Leroy, in 1970, Stacey had abruptly left town for unknown reasons and gone to California for a period of time. Only after she returned to Kentucky did she contact Leroy and tell him about their baby son and how she had placed him for adoption in California.

Leroy was from a wealthy tobacco farming family. Once they found out about the situation, his family had wanted to find the baby and raise it, but they didn't know who to contact until it was too late, and the adoption had already gone through. We could only conclude that either Stacey had lied to the adoption agency to cover her tracks, or the agency didn't want to have to deal with getting a relinquishment from Leroy, so they just wrote him out of the picture.

Leroy told us that after telling him about the baby, Stacey broke off their relationship completely, but came back to their high school and finished her senior year. She ended up marrying the football coach and divorcing him later. Leroy knew of several other marriages and divorces that Stacey went through, but most importantly, he knew her current last name and we were able to locate her with our databases. She was still living in the same small town that she and Leroy grew up in!

Let Sleeping Dogs Lie

When we called Stacey, she was very uncooperative. She had just recently remarried and said it would be an embarrassment to her new family. She was just not interested in a reunion and wanted to let sleeping dogs lie. She wasn't open to giving us any information, not even her family's health history. She'd married into money and her new stepson was a noted celebrity. She didn't want to rock the boat. We never called her again. Jon also honored her wishes and has never contacted her to this day.

With Leroy's permission, we gave his phone number to Jon and told him to go ahead and call. It was a lot for Jon, after all those years, to realize his search was finally over and that it had been worth the wait. Here he was, at last, with his birthfather waiting for him at the other end of a telephone line. He called Leroy and they arranged for Jon to fly out and spend a week together in Leroy's hometown.

Jon got the time off from his job in information technology quality control, and went to meet Leroy. He flew into Lexington, Kentucky then caught a commuter plane to the beautiful, rural town.

Where it All Started

At the airport they bumped into each other while Jon was coming out of the men's room. Leroy looked at him and asked, *"Are you Jon?"* and Jon looked back and asked, *"Are you Leroy?"* Neither of them really knew if it was because they'd recognized each other or it was just because it was such a small place. Leroy was a recovering alcoholic but had a six-pack of beer as a welcome gift for Jon! They drove to Leroy's house out in the country, where Jon met Sandy, Leroy's second wife, who was happy to meet Jon and turned out to be very hospitable.

That Sunday Leroy took Jon to church, where Jon was shocked to discover that the entire congregation was expecting him! After the service, he stood outside and greeted what seemed like the whole town. Jon's (paternal) half sister, Sammi, was also there to meet him.

Stacey didn't show up at church that day. In such a small town, there was no way she wouldn't have heard that Jon was going to be there. But she never came.

Later, Leroy took Jon to a friend's house, to look at old photos, and talk about old times—and to show off his newly found birth son. Another friend came over, a woman who knew Stacey well. She told Jon that he looked just like his mother. Jon wondered if this woman had been sent by Stacey, and whether she reported back to her about him. It's a mystery he may never know the answer to.

Jon knew that Stacey and her husband owned the local music store. Jon played in a band in his spare time and had a lifelong love of music. He wanted to visit the store incognito, just to get a glimpse of the woman who'd carried him for nine months. But now he realized he would probably be recognized and decided not to do it.

He spent the rest of his visit hanging out with Leroy, meeting people and visiting the graves and important landmarks of his paternal ancestors. One memorable occasion was when Leroy took him to the place where he had been conceived. It was the town's make-out spot way off down a country road. Jon videotaped the spot for posterity. After all, how many people, adopted or not, get to see the actual place of their conception?

Culture Clash

It was a long road from California to Kentucky. Leroy was very warm and accepting towards Jon, and Jon felt a real affection for Leroy, but they lived in different worlds. In some ways though, Jon and Leroy were quite similar. Leroy also previously had addiction problems and a tough time with relationships. While meeting Leroy might have in some sense explained to Jon where some of his characteristics came from, it didn't solve all his problems as he had hoped. But it did provide Jon with an experience that was vital to him: Closure.

You Only Get One Life

After reuniting with Leroy, Jon saw how he'd gotten stuck thinking that everything would change for the better once he'd found his birthparents. He'd built up this fantasy that this reunion was going to be his saving grace. Not knowing his heritage was the root, he thought, of all his problems. Now that the mystery was gone once and forever, Jon was left with himself, and with a new capacity to take responsibility for his own life.

> "The whole experience freed me in a way. I felt I had the strength or the wherewithal I needed to come to grips with what I had to do to change things."

Today, Jon has been drug free for five years. He stopped abusing substances immediately after his reunion with Leroy. He joined a men's therapy group that helped with his emotional ups and downs. He married his long time girlfriend and they have a darling one year-old son. He has moved forward with his life and made the necessary changes to end his struggles and begin to thrive. We are honored that we were able to be part of his success story.

CHAPTER 11

Kathy's Search

A Lifetime of Mixed Messages

From the beginning, Kathy's case was complicated, and remains so to this day. Our search for her birthparents lasted five years and at the time of writing is still not wholly complete. We located her birthmother's family, but could never get valid clues to her birthfather's identity. At a certain point both Kathy and our agency had to accept the possibility that the final bit of information so needed to close her case might never be revealed to us.

Kathy's Lost Years

When Kathy, a soft-spoken, well educated woman in her fifties, first called our office, she was understandably nervous. She was born in California, but wasn't even sure that she had been adopted or not. Since she was born in California, we were confident that we could easily determine the answer for her.

Kathy faxed us a copy of her legal birth certificate, and we were fairly certain by the delayed issue date that it was an amended birth certificate, and that Kathy was indeed adopted. We then checked her birth certificate information on the California Birth Index. This index routinely lists births by date, and then alphabetically by the mother's maiden name. If someone was adopted, they would have two entries: first under their original certificate information, and then under their amended certificate information. However, during a few years in the middle 1940's, the California Birth Index only listed the amended birth certificate—the original birth information was completely deleted from the index. We were disappointed to find out that 1946 was one of those years—known in Californian adoption circles as the 'Lost Years.'

We called and informed Kathy that from looking at the birth certificate she had faxed, we were almost certain that it was amended and that she had been adopted. Then we explained that the 1946 index did not list her *original* birth certificate information as it would have in other years. *"That's just the story of my life,"* she said.

Kathy was our first client who had been born in those years. We never did get a clear answer as to why a few years of adoptees' original birth records were removed from the California birth index, but we were clear regarding Kathy's case—we didn't have the typical information for starting a California search with information from the index: the adoptee's original name; maiden name for the birthmother; and the birthfather's last name if he had been named on the original birth certificate.

A Lifetime of Mixed Messages

What stood out in our conversations with Kathy was that throughout her childhood, Kathy really didn't know if she had truly been adopted. This was the result of her parents giving mixed messages to her ever since she was old enough to understand what they were saying. Many times they taunted her, saying that she was an unwanted child, that her birthfather had wanted to keep her, but her birthmother hadn't cared about her at all, and had given her away.

Other times they would try to convince her that she hadn't been adopted at all and was their own biological child. Kathy never knew for sure whether she was really born to her parents; legally adopted; or actually stolen from another family. She just knew her place in this family was precarious, and she felt that she didn't belong at all. As you can imagine, this kind of mental and emotional abuse took its toll on Kathy, mentally & physically. She reported suffering with seizures from stress since the age of seventeen.

Kathy now had a keen desire to solve the mystery of who her birth family really was. Kathy's mother died years ago, and her father had just recently passed away, and the truth had never been told to her, even as an adult. Though more often than not, adoptive parents truly want the child they bring into their home, there are those instances when adoptive parents turn out to be abusive. This was the case with Kathy, who experienced a spectrum of abuse, from sexual touching at the hands of her father, to her mother's emotional cruelty. This fact made it all the more poignant to us when she told us that she had moved in with her father at the end of his life, nursing him through his final illness and making sure he wouldn't be alone. Somehow over the years Kathy had acquired compassion for others, even though she did not learn it from her parents.

The Perfect Little Girl

While growing up, Kathy carried the feeling that her parents must have gone out and bought a baby, just like you would a refrigerator. She never could understand why they'd even bothered with her. The abuse she received from her parents gave her the impression at a very early age that she'd turned out to be a big disappointment to them. When she was little, one of the conflicting stories they told her was that before adopting her, they'd looked at a lot of babies, but she was the special one because she was so perfect. But that image soon faded:

> "Around 3 years old I began to act out in very unusual behaviors my parents weren't expecting from their *'perfect little girl'*—I was far too independent for their liking. I wouldn't listen and I already understood deep down that the 'perfect' façade they were presenting to the world just wasn't real."

Kathy ran away from home at ten years of age, the same year she first had sex. Her adventures landed her on probation and by the age of 12 she'd become a heavy drinker. At age 15, Kathy bore a healthy daughter, Jill, and she was forced by her parents to relinquish her baby for adoption. Kathy recalls:

> "After Jill was born my parents had a fake funeral for her and invited all of our family because no matter what, they were going to make sure that no one knew the truth of what had really happened and the hand they played in it."

Kathy was forced to go along with this story, and it just added to her turmoil and sense of unreality about what was true in her life and what was made up by her parents.

Addiction and Confusion

A year later at age 16, Kathy became pregnant again, and out of desperation married an 18 year old who was not the father of her baby. She was then tricked by her parents and her husband into entering a home for unwed mothers. The betrayal ran deep, because her husband had promised her that even though this baby wasn't his, they would keep it. After her baby was born, Kathy's husband and parents immediately teamed up and initiated arrangements to place the baby girl for adoption. They checked Kathy out of the hospital the day after the birth and drove her home; leaving behind the baby she had named Kathleen.

After being forced to sign the relinquishment papers for the baby, Kathy felt she had nothing else to loose, and started binge drinking and experimenting with street drugs. Her hatred and distrust of her husband became extreme; however she continued to live with him because it was better than living in her parents' home again.

Kathy's substance abuse escalated over the next months, and she became addicted to heroin as well as alcohol. One night when she came home drunk and high and unable to fight back, her husband attacked and raped her. The result was the birth of a son—Zak—who was born two months early and had to live in hospital for a month before being released to her. By then, she was 18 years old, of legal age, and no one could take Zak away from her.

Here's how Kathy characterizes the confusion of her early adulthood:

> "At 20 years of age I enrolled in *Synanon* for drug rehab and remained for the next five and a half years. By then I had lived a lifetime. I saw shrinks for years not knowing what the hell had happened to me to turn me so wild. The whole thing about my dad touching me didn't come out until the late 1980's and still I can't even think clearly about it."

Years of therapy turned out to be good for Kathy. She learned about the connection between familial sexual abuse and her years of wild, self-destructive behavior. Along with the other rehab patients, she talked about her parents and her early life over and over again until at a certain point she realized she could no longer blame anyone else for the decisions she had made:

> "I think deep inside my soul was the thought that if my own mother doesn't want me, like my mother didn't want me, then there's that feeling that there must be something terribly wrong with you. I feel this is what was at the core of my endless searching for approval and

> love in all the wrong ways. I wanted my real mother, and I prayed that the woman who raised me was *not* my real mother."

In rehab, Kathy met a man who helped her get out from under the influence of her adopted family, and though it wasn't all roses by any means, she stayed with this man for the next 15 years.

The Quest for an Original Birth Certificate

As a first step to finding Kathy's birthparents, we wrote a formal letter to the State of California Mutual Registry for her. We knew that if they didn't handle the adoption process, they'd at least be able to point us in the right direction to find out more. Just like Kathy's life, nothing seemed to come easy in this search. The Registry lost her application and she had to submit another one. Eight months passed before we had an answer.

Kathy was born in San Diego. However, Los Angeles County handled her adoption process, because that was where her adoptive parents lived at the time. We contacted the Los Angeles County Post Adoption Services, but the Non-Identifying Information they provided turned out to be almost useless as they weren't able to provide first or last names for either birthparent.

Next, with Kathy's permission, we petitioned the Los Angeles Superior Court to open her closed adoption file. We cited Kathy's health issues and the fact that Kathy had grown children who had the right to know their medical history. Kathy had her doctor confirm that she was on medication and that knowing her medical history was an urgent matter for her and her children. We proposed to the court that at 55 years of age, there was no danger of Kathy being an infringement on her birthparents' life. Both her adopted parents were deceased and that meant they could not be harmed or disturbed in any way by her making contact with her birthparents. It took a whole year before Los Angeles County released Kathy's file.

While we waited for the records to be opened, we searched for Kathy's second birthdaughter, Kathleen, and found her very quickly—the same week we began the search. We made contact with Kathleen, and gently explained that her birthmother was willing to open the door to contact. Kathleen was overjoyed to discover that her birthmother wanted to know her! In talking with Kathleen, she told us that her parents had divorced when she was very small, and she was raised entirely by her father, so she had never really had the experience of a mother figure in her life. She was married and had recently given birth to her first child, and she welcomed Kathy into their lives. This was a doubly blessed reunion on both sides—years before she'd hired us, Kathy had contact with her first daughter, Jill. Jill had not been particularly responsive to Kathy, so Kathleen's warmth and acceptance was an especially welcome gift.

Original Birth Certificate Released

When we finally had Kathy's unsealed adoption file in front of us, the birth family member's names were blacked out, as is often the case. But as a stroke of luck for us, they'd also released Kathy's original birth certificate with all information intact. It revealed her birthmother's full name, age and address at the time.

Kathy finally knew the name of the woman who had given her life—Shirley San Martin. The file described Shirley as a pretty, well-groomed young woman of refined appearance. Though slightly reserved, she was easy for the agency to interview and answered their questions freely and frankly about everything, until questioned about the birthfather. She gave some personal details about him and his family, but refused to divulge his name.

Shirley was born December 6, 1922 in Long Beach. Her parents were American born and of French and English descent. She completed a year of high school in San Diego and went on to work as a secretary. In 1941 she married a Mr. Jenson in Yuma, Arizona, where he was stationed in the military. Two years later she bore him a son, even though by this time their marriage was in trouble and it seemed unlikely they would stay together. When Shirley's husband was shipped overseas in 1944, they agreed not to make any decisions about their situation until he returned. Shirley moved back to San Diego and lived with her mother while he was away.

Mr. Jenson returned from the service in 1946, and he and Shirley mutually agreed that they should get a divorce as soon as possible. Shirley went to Reno and filed for divorce, as Nevada had lax residency requirements, and divorces were finalized very quickly. It was not until she had secured the divorce in September 1946 that Shirley revealed to Mr. Jensen that she was pregnant by another man. Kathy was born two months later on December 12th. Shirley went to extreme lengths to try to use her ex-husband's name as the father on Kathy's birth certificate. Though Mr. Jenson had been quite willing to divorce Shirley—he remarried very soon after the papers were final—he was furious about her pregnancy and did not want his name listed as the father of a child that wasn't his. He remained angry and rude during the numerous attempts of the adoption agency to call him regarding his status on Kathy's birth certificate. Shirley even went so far as to hire an attorney to try to convince Mr. Jenson to allow his name to be listed on the birth certificate. He flatly refused to have anything to do with the situation.

What's in a name?

After their failed attempts, the agency never contacted Mr. Jenson again concerning the matter. When Kathy was born, her original birth certificate was filled out with '*Refused*' put in all the spaces for the father's information, except for '*Father's Race,' which* stated '*White.*' But she was actually listed as 'Unnamed Jensen.' Why did Shirley go to such lengths to keep Kathy's biological father's name off the birth certificate? Why didn't she just give her the last name of San Martin, her own maiden name? We'll never know for sure.

After the birth, Shirley never saw or held Kathy, she just wanted reassurance that the infant was perfect and healthy. In consenting to the choice of adoptive parents, Shirley trusted her doctor's opinion of them. Unfortunately for all concerned, this doctor was clearly no great judge of character. Of Kathy's adoptive parents, he noted in the file: "I think they are fine, high class people."

Facts About the Birth Father According to Shirley

The following is an excerpt from the adoption file concerning Kathy's birthfather:

> The mother preferred not to give the father's name and agent did not press the matter. She stated that he was a Naval Lieutenant at the time she knew him. She described him as being a typical southern gentleman. He was quiet, friendly and well mannered and everyone liked him. He is about twenty-six years of age, American born, of Spanish origin. He is slender, 5 feet 8 inches tall, with brunette coloring, dark brown eyes and hair and a Catholic.

In reference to Shirley's pregnancy, it was reported that the birthfather was at first sympathetic and wanted to help, but then he became frightened that she would 'stick him.' According to the record, he left the Navy and went into the diplomatic service, traveling to Canada and Mexico. He did offer at times to pay for some expenses, but Shirley refused to involve him.

It was noted in the papers that all of this information had been disclosed to Kathy's adoptive parents at the time of the adoption. The willingness of the birthfather to pay for some of the birthmother's expenses was used against Kathy when she was young—her adoptive parents had often told her that her birthfather had wanted to keep her, but that it had been her birthmother who hadn't wanted her and had given Kathy away. For a long time Kathy lived under the illusion that her birthfather loved and wanted her and that it was her birthmother who had wholly and completely rejected her.

Kathy's image of her birthfather, based on the stories she had been told by her parents, was now somewhat different after reading the information Shirley gave about him. Here is what the file revealed to her from the caseworkers notes:

> The mother seemed a little bitter and disillusioned from her experience. She said that she could not understand the father, 'since he poses as a good Catholic and goes to Church every Sunday, so why isn't he living up to his beliefs?'

Was Shirley's bitterness the reason she worked so hard to keep the birthfather's name off Kathy's certificate? Did he somehow threaten her and demand that she not use his name? Were there other, untold reasons why she pushed Mr. Jenson to get him to consent to be named as the father? We've discussed this issue many times, with and without Kathy, but to this day it remains a mystery.

Tracing the Road to Shirley

Shirley's last name of San Martin was very unusual and this enabled us to locate her almost immediately—we identified and found her the same day we received the unsealed records and original birth certificate from the court. She was living in Hawaii with her sister Margie and Margie's husband. Over the next few days, we made several calls and left messages, but no one responded.

Finally Judy called them very early one morning and Shirley's sister Margie answered. She told Judy that Shirley had been hospitalized right at the time she'd first started calling. Shirley was not doing well, and Margie said that if Judy had something to discuss with Shirley, she would have to let Margie relay it to her, as she was too ill to take calls at the hospital. Judy felt this was the only chance she would have to get through to Shirley, so contrary to our policy of strict confidentiality, Judy told Margie that we were calling on behalf of Shirley's birthdaughter. Margie suddenly became very formal and reserved when given this information—and Judy could tell she wasn't pleased in the least to get this call. Margie said that if Judy sent proof through the mail concerning Kathy's relationship to Shirley, she *might* consider speaking about it further, on her sister's behalf.

We mailed Margie a copy of Kathy's original birth certificate, assuming that she would take it to the hospital to show Shirley that her birthdaughter was looking for her. Ten days went by and we never heard a word. Finally, Margie called to tell us that Shirley had died of uterine cancer and that she had not been able to bring herself to tell her about Kathy while she was so sick. We were shocked. There we were, ready to set up contact between Kathy and her birthmother, and now it would never happen, due in part to Margie's interference.

A Hawaiian Funeral and a Stubborn Sister

After delivering this devastating news about Shirley's death, Margie described the funeral to us and we passed the information on to Kathy. Paul Jenson, Kathy's half brother, had married a Hawaiian lady years ago, and all their children and grandchildren were at Shirley's funeral. Along with them, a slew of cousins and nephews also attended the traditional Hawaiian funeral ceremony. Margie said it was so beautiful; with the sun setting on the water, the entire funeral party canoed out in the ocean to witness the scattering of Shirley's ashes, and everyone had brought a flower lei to toss into the water to honor her. Margie wanted us to let Kathy know that she had placed a second lei in the water on her behalf as well, although she didn't tell anyone who the lei was being placed for.

Once we'd recounted the details of Shirley's funeral to Kathy, she decided to contact Margie by telephone, and left a message when no one answered. After a short period of no response, she left further messages, and then wrote a letter, but still, Margie never replied. After waiting a few weeks, it was clear that Margie had no intention of responding to Kathy's messages or letter. We had already located Shirley's son Paul, but had not yet contacted him; we wanted to give Margie the chance to tell him about Kathy. But we felt now was the time for Kathy to call her brother, even though she was afraid he would rebuff her as Margie had. Surprisingly to Kathy, Paul was delighted to hear from her and was thrilled to know that he had a sister who wanted to meet him. His whole family was excited, too, and got on the phone to warmly welcome Kathy into their lives. And he was not as shocked about Kathy's call as she had expected. Paul told Kathy that once their mother's funeral was over, he turned to Margie and said, "Okay, Auntie, where's my sister?" He'd heard rumors over the years through his uncles that he had a sister somewhere, and he'd heard his mother mention something about a *daughter* on her deathbed. He also had noticed Margie place the extra lei. Still, Margie refused to answer his questions or discuss the matter any further.

Kathy immediately booked a flight to Hawaii, and went for a twelve day visit. Paul, his wife Grayce, and their children all confirmed that on the day of her death, Shirley had asked for her saying, "Where is my daughter?" Even though Margie was present during this conversation, she never opened her mouth to let her sister know that her daughter was looking for her.

During Kathy's visit, Paul brought out a photograph of Shirley with an unknown soldier, a lieutenant in the Navy. They both agreed that this man was probably Kathy's father. Paul had tried to get Margie to open up about it, but she maintained her silence. In fact, all attempts Kathy made while she was in Hawaii to meet Margie were ignored; Margie always had a 'previous engagement.'

Speculating About Margie's Silence

Kathy, Paul, and his family discussed Margie's puzzling behavior over and over again. Paul and Grayce each individually approached her and pleaded with her to tell them the name of Kathy's birthfather with no success. Why was Margie so tight-lipped? We can only speculate.

One possible reason is the era Margie and Shirley were brought up in—an environment of shame around so many things, especially young girls, pregnancies and family honor. Out of wedlock pregnancy was simply not spoken of.

We wondered if there was something about Kathy's biological father that Margie just didn't want anyone to know—was he married with a family, or undesirable in some other way? Such issues could still exist as a badge of shame for Margie, especially if she knew that this was how Shirley felt about it.

Of course, there's always the possibility that Margie knew nothing at all, and she was hurt that Shirley had never confided in her about having a baby out of wedlock years ago.

The Cat is Beyond Out of the Bag

Kathy's last letter of appeal to Margie, sent in December of 2006, included the photograph of Shirley with the Naval Lieutenant. Here is a portion of what she wrote:

> *...As they say, the cat is beyond out of the bag here. You could give me a gift that would help me in ways you couldn't even imagine, peace of mind for starters. I cannot think of any reason that keeping my father's name from me would benefit anyone at this point, 60 years after my birth. I also cannot imagine you being anything other than a loving, kind woman, so please, can you find it in your heart to give me the grace of knowing my birthfather's name? I promise this is the last time I will beg and plead with you to help me, I will never write or contact you again...*

Margie never responded to Kathy's plea, and now will never have a change of heart and break her silence, as she passed away soon after receiving this letter. Sometimes we wonder how things could be different for Kathy if we'd been able to reach Shirley before her death. After all those years of separation, we'd missed making the connection by just a matter of days. Maybe they both would have gotten a measure of peace of mind by connecting before Shirley's death. Or maybe she'd have been just as uncooperative as Margie. She might have refused contact and even blocked Kathy from meeting Paul.

Though Kathy is still in the dark about her birthfather, she has the blessing of a close relationship with her brother and his wife. In fact, due to his serious health needs, Paul and Grayce moved to California and have been in constant contact with Kathy the last few years. Paul waited months for a lung transplant, which he finally received, and is now doing very well. While Kathy's relationship with her birthdaughter Jill didn't turn out as she had hoped, she has a very close relationship with her son, Zak, and her birthdaughter Kathleen, for which she is immensely grateful.

Kathy didn't get all the answers she was looking for, but she has found peace in finally knowing that she really was adopted, and that although she missed meeting her birthmother Shirley, she was on her mind and in her heart until the day she died.

Sometimes the book of secrets doesn't open entirely. Sometimes, secrets die with the birthmother or other members of the birth family, and you just have to accept that you're out of luck. Or maybe, when all is said and done, you're in luck. You just never know.

CHAPTER 12

Kelly's Search

Mysterious Beginnings

A mystery surrounded Kelly from the moment of her birth in the spring of 1964. Her birthmother, along with the doctor who was to deliver her at a hospital in Santa Rosa, California, had prepared for her adoption long before her birth. And Gary, her soon-to-be adoptive father, knew of those plans well before she was born.

Knowing that his wife Jackie very much longed for a child, Gary had told her that he knew of a baby that would soon be available for adoption. In later years, many questions swirled throughout Kelly's family: How did her father know about the baby that was available for adoption? Was it through the doctor or the attorney that handled the private adoption? Or did he hear about Kelly through someone he knew?

All through the years, some of Gary's family members would insinuate that they knew the circumstances surrounding Kelly's birth, although it was never made clear to Kelly or to her mother just what they knew. This was very confusing and upsetting to both of them.

Regardless of the circumstances and the questions, Kelly fulfilled the dreams and prayers of her mother Jackie, who took her in her arms when she was only three days old and held her in her heart forever.

A Privileged Childhood?

When Kelly's adoption was finalized, Jackie and Gary took their new baby and moved back to their home state of Mississippi, where Kelly has lived ever since. When she started pre-school, she heard many scary stories about 'step-mothers' and she asked her mom if *she* was her stepmother. Her mother decided it was time to tell Kelly she was adopted, before someone else did—and maybe in not as gentle a way as Jackie would.

Like most adoptees, Kelly was told that she was chosen and, her mother added, that made her 'more special' than other children. Kelly had no idea that one conversation would so deeply impact her entire life.

The conversation left her with a feeling of privilege. She told her amazing news to all of her little friends, and then tried to convince them of how 'special' she was. She spent much of her life trying to convince herself as well.

Kelly was eight years old when her parents ended a long, unhappy marriage of turbulence and violence. She, along with her mother, became estranged from her father. She has always felt that her adoption might have been a last ditch effort to save that marriage.

After the divorce, Jackie received full custody of Kelly. Jackie turned to her church for comfort and support and there she reunited with Bart, a childhood friend. After dating a few years, they got married when Kelly was ten years old.

After her mother remarried, Kelly felt like she had lost her special place with her mother and she turned to her maternal grandmother for comfort and guidance. 'Granny' became a very important force in her life, and it was during this time that Kelly started to wonder about her birth family.

Whom did she look like? Did she have brothers and sisters? Kelly imagined being the daughter of star-crossed lovers, maybe royalty or even movie stars. As she got older, Kelly started to question the circumstances of her adoption as well. Did her birthmother ever think of her on her birthday? Birthdays became days of sadness and longing for Kelly.

Kelly knew her birthmother's name was 'Carolyn Ann Wilburn' as it was listed on her adoption decree. Another name 'Lee' was also listed, but she didn't know how that fit into the scenario.

Adoption decrees are almost never given to the adoptive parents with the birthparents' names listed on them, so Kelly had a rare gift to help her in her search.

Birthday Blunder

On her 17th birthday, Kelly, with the encouragement and help of her best friend, got on the phone and the two girls took turns calling Santa Rosa, California directory assistance until they got telephone listings for every Wilburn in the area. They then called each number and asked for Carolyn. One lady said she had a cousin by the name of Carolyn Wilburn, who lived in Turlock, California, but she would not give them her phone number.

They called Turlock directory assistance and got a phone number for Carolyn Wilburn, and with shaking hands Kelly made the call. A young girl answered and when Kelly asked for Carolyn, the girl yelled for her mother to come to the phone. Kelly's heart jumped! '*I have a sister!*' she thought. Kelly was convinced she had found her birthmother. But when she told her story to the lady, the lady very rudely told her she was mistaken, that her name was Carolyn Marie, not Ann, and she hung up on her. Kelly was devastated and couldn't bring herself to make any more calls.

This is a prime example of why we always advise our clients to allow a mediator to make the first contact. Many negative words can be spoken out of fear and surprise. Or, as often happens, the person called might deny they are the person being sought, when indeed they are. (This was not the case with the lady in Turlock.) Shock, fear and other feelings can cause a triad member to react harshly to an unexpected phone call. An experienced mediator, as an impartial party, can be very reassuring and no threat to their privacy. The mediator can keep communications open until both parties have come to a decision about contact.

Troubled Years Ahead

The next ten years brought turmoil between Kelly and her mother, as Kelly was determined to live life on her own terms. Jackie was a rather stern woman whose life revolved around her church, home and family, while Kelly was somewhat of a 'free spirit' who wanted to explore and experience more of the world. She started college and dropped out several times, worked a string of different jobs, and finally joined the Army. She felt very different from the rest of her family and carried with her a deep sadness of not knowing her biological origins.

At the age of 23, Kelly met and married Andy and two years later, became pregnant. She was excited to begin her new family and dreamed of the beautiful life they would have together. Tragically her baby, a little boy, was born with a very rare genetic disorder and died before he turned two years old, a painful loss that still haunts her to this day.

Kelly became determined to find out who had passed on this killer gene to her beloved son and she began to search for her birth family again. She first registered with every adoption registry in the US.

Her mother, who was very supportive and helpful with her search, obtained the name of the attorney who handled her adoption, and Kelly began to appeal to the State of California to open her adoption records. After two years, and with the help of her son's geneticists, Kelly received a document that had both her birthmother and birthfather's signatures. She finally had both her birthparents' names. Her birthfather's name was Nathan D. Lee.

Reunion with Paternal Family

At this point, Kelly contacted us and sent us all the information that she had gathered. We went to work and traced Nathan D. Lee to Las Vegas, Nevada and obtained his last known address. Unfortunately, with further research we learned that he had died five years earlier. This news totally devastated Kelly. She felt that she had lost the only two people that she knew of that were a flesh and blood part of her—her son and her father.

The next day we obtained an obituary for Nathan, which listed Nathan's widow, Sally. Within 24 hours, we had located Sally Lee and obtained her current address and phone number.

A Widow Speaks

Once we had a phone number, we spoke with Sally, who, although in extremely poor health, was very gracious. She had some knowledge of Kelly's birth and would be happy to tell her anything she could. When Kelly called her, Sally told her that Nathan had fathered three daughters (two besides Kelly, and all with different women). She also said that Nathan had a genius IQ, and that he and his mother both were manic-depressive. This news made Kelly realize how deep genetics run since she herself had been diagnosed as manic-depressive two years before.

According to his wife, just before he died, Nathan told her that he had a very strong feeling that one of his daughters needed him and was searching for him. His death occurred at almost the same time that Kelly felt the urgent need to start the search for her biological family.

The Good News

Sally then gave Kelly the news that made her heart sing—she had a half-brother! Nathan and Sally had one son together, Kent, who lived in Texas, and she gave Kelly his phone number. Kelly immediately called Kent, who was both surprised and elated to know he had a sister. He wanted to come that very weekend to meet her.

Kelly got so excited she couldn't sleep. She bought new clothes, colored her hair, prepared food she thought Kent would like and scrubbed the bathroom floor with a toothbrush in readiness for his visit!

When Kent arrived that weekend, it was very obvious they were of the same genetic line. They looked so much alike they could have been twins, and Kent's girlfriend, who had come along with him, exclaimed, "Oh my God, look at Kelly's hands, they are just like yours!"

Kent had brought pictures of their father, and told Kelly stories about him. The only things he knew about their two sisters were their names, Rebecca and Natalie. Rebecca was eight years older than Kelly, and Natalie was four years older. Nathan had been married to Natalie's mother. Nathan had not married Rebecca's mother, a showgirl in Las Vegas.

Kent and Kelly have maintained a close relationship and stay in touch regularly. Kent has moved to California, and is now a very busy and successful record producer who travels extensively. Kelly feels a deep kinship with him and they talk on the phone several times a month. She is very proud of her brother and his professional achievements.

A Sister Found

We easily found Natalie, one of Kelly's half-sisters, living in Prescott, Arizona. She wasn't home when we called and we spoke with her husband. He indicated that Natalie would not be interested in a relationship. We were proud of Kelly for staying so levelheaded in the face of this news. Kelly did not call again, but instead wrote Natalie a letter that year at Christmas and Natalie responded the next month. She did not close the door on getting to know Kelly, but did not express a lot of enthusiasm either. A few years later, Kelly came out to Arizona and spent the day with Natalie. They got along very well and will likely have a very stable relationship in the future. We have never searched for Rebecca, as we have no clues as to her or her mother's identity.

Maternal Family a Mismatch

After a very extensive and difficult search we finally located a maternal half-sister of Kelly's, who was married and lived in California. She also had been placed for adoption by their birthmother. It was much later that we found Kelly's birthmother, Carolyn, who was reluctant at first to make contact with Kelly, but later relented and called her. They met and she told Kelly that she also had a son that was raised by his grandmother (her mother). Kelly has now met all of Carolyn's side of the family and they have visited back and forth a few times. They get in touch once or twice a year; however, Kelly does not seem to have a lot in common with any of the maternal side of her birth family and has not formed strong attachments with any of them.

Kelly's One True Mother

Kelly's mother Jackie supported her in all of her search efforts and when Carolyn came to visit Kelly, Jackie greeted her and made every effort to make her feel welcome, even though it was obvious they were two very different women. Like any mother and daughter, Kelly and Jackie agreed on some things and disagreed on others. But there has always been a strong bond and deep love between them. Kelly says she wishes she could have made her mom really know and understand ***"that she is my one true mother."***

Jackie and Granny have both since passed away, but Kelly says the teachings they instilled in her have made her strong, and, in many ways she becomes more like them every day. She and Andy have a beautiful, healthy son who is now four years old and the joy of their lives. It was never determined that their first child's genetic disorder was inherited from either of Kelly's biological parents. Still, Kelly now feels content in knowing the answers to many of the questions that had plagued her since childhood.

CHAPTER 13

MARY LOU'S SEARCH

The Silver Lining

When Mary Lou came to us through the Arizona Confidential Intermediary Program, she was happily married with two adopted children of her own. Her husband, Dave, completely supported her desire to find her birthmother and put to rest all the years of wondering about the circumstances of her adoption.

Mary Lou's adoptive parents, Paul and Cindy, had one son, Clark, when they discovered that they would not be able to have any more children. Not long after finding this out, Cindy's mother was at a bridge game where she learned of a local family who was placing a baby girl for adoption. That game of cards changed Mary Lou's life forever.

The Chosen Child

Paul and Cindy were ecstatic with the news of a little girl needing a family and quickly made arrangements to adopt her. Two days later they drove to a mutual meeting spot to pick up their new baby and bring her home. Mary Lou was about nine months old at that time. She recalls:

> "I became part of a wonderful, kind and loving new family. I always felt secure and loved by my family, and was never treated any differently than my brother Clark."

Mary Lou remembers her parents telling her throughout her childhood that she was very special and that they had 'chosen' her for their daughter. Mary Lou had asked them if they had met her birth parents, but they hadn't, and didn't know very much about them. Mary Lou was satisfied with their answer, and didn't think much more about it.

An Imprint of Loss

As Mary Lou approached her teenage years, tragedy struck her family. During a trip to the Canary Islands, her parents were involved in an airplane crash. While Paul escaped with minor burns, Cindy was severely burned all over her body. She spent one month in a burn treatment center before dying at the age of 36. Paul, Clark and Mary Lou were devastated. All three were left with an enormous void in their lives.

Mary Lou had feelings of anger and confusion as to why her mother had been taken from her. Cindy had been the most wonderful mother to her and Clark, and the loss left them aching. Over time, with the loving support of their father, the family began to heal their grief and start living again, without Cindy.

A New Love in Her Life

The loss of her mother brought all of Mary Lou's thoughts and curiosity about her birthmother to the surface. During the next several years, she wondered "what did this woman look like and did she ever think about me?"

Meanwhile a new love came into her life. At 26 years of age, Mary Lou met Dave, who she felt to be her soul mate:

> "His unconditional love filled a part of my heart that had been empty since my mother's death. He was my angel sent straight from heaven."

After three years of marriage, Dave and Mary Lou decided to start a family. This decision brought on a roller coaster ride of emotions after they learned that Mary Lou suffered from endometriosis. Mary Lou had three surgical procedures in the following year, but still had no success becoming pregnant. Next, they turned to fertility treatments, undergoing several months of costly prescriptions and procedures. Still, Mary Lou could not get pregnant and they decided that the time had come to investigate the option of adopting children.

Coming Full Circle

As Mary Lou and Dave searched for a baby to adopt, questions rose again in Mary Lou about her own adoption. What were her birthmother's circumstances and reasons for placing her for adoption? Now that the tables were turned, and she was the one seeking to adopt, she couldn't help but want to know her own personal history. Mary Lou says:

> "This is where my story of adoption comes full circle. I always believed in the miracle of adoption because of the wonderful gift both my families had given to me. I never

> thought it would be the same way that Dave and I would build our whole family as well."

When they met the birthmother of their first child, Kevin, Mary Lou greatly admired the woman's decision to give her child a better life than she herself was capable of providing. Three months after bringing Kevin home, Mary Lou's father died following a three-year battle with cancer. She felt he had hung on long enough to see her happy with her baby. His illness and death made her realize the importance of knowing her own biological family medical history.

A few years later, when Dave and Mary Lou were ready to adopt again, they developed an extremely close relationship with the birthmother of their second baby. Dave and Mary Lou were in the delivery room during the birth, and the three of them went through it all together. Mary Lou began to imagine what it must have been like for her birthmother: Was it difficult to give her baby up after carrying her for nine months? Did she grieve for Mary Lou once she was gone? Whenever she asked Dave what he thought, his reply was the always the same—"*Why don't we find out?*"

Why Don't We Find Out?

Finally, Mary Lou felt ready to move forward with the search for her birthmother. Dave started by speaking to their adoption caseworker, who felt it would be beneficial for Mary Lou. Through their adoption caseworker, Dave obtained a list of Confidential Intermediaries in Arizona and Mary Lou chose Kristen to be her CI.

Once Kristen agreed to take the case, all kinds of emotions broke loose in Mary Lou—especially strong was the fear of rejection. What if her birthmother didn't want to know her? What if she had a new family to whom she'd never mentioned Mary Lou's existence? What if, what if, what if?

After receiving the required paperwork, Kristen walked Mary

Lou through the CI program and explained the order in which things would proceed. Kristen reassured her that she would be there for her no matter what the outcome.

Mary Lou did not have any information about her adoption beyond her birth date, birthplace and the hospital in which she was born. Kristen, as a C.I., was able to view the complete adoption file, and obtain Mary Lou's original birth certificate through the courts. The birthmother's first name was Allison, and her maiden name was so unusual that it was fairly easy to identify her.

Because of the regulations of the Confidential Intermediary Program, Kristen was not allowed to tell Mary Lou what her birthmother's name was or where she was from, but she was able to tell her that she had contacted her birthmother's mother. But then Kristen added that the grandmother had also revealed some bad news: her birthmother had died years ago. Mary Lou recalls:

> "As I heard those words coming through the phone, all the blood in my body seemed to rush to my feet and I felt like I was going to pass out."

A Sign in the Sky

It was as though the wind had been taken out of her sails and all she could think to do was sit down and cry. Kristen stayed on the line with her for a while, comforting her by telling her of an option to get more information by applying for a grandparent search through the CIP. Later, with Dave's help, Mary Lou came to grips with the intensity of her emotions. Mary Lou remembers that time:

> "I prayed to my father and asked him to show me that things were going to be okay. As I opened my eyes, there was a cloud formation in the sky in the clear shape of a cross. I knew right then there was a bigger plan for me and I had to continue to go after it."

The day after her devastating news, Mary Lou called Kristen and instructed her to re-file the C.I. papers, this time directed to her biological grandmother. Kristen was happy that she would be able to once again contact the birth grandmother, Jo, and already knew that she would be willing to give Mary Lou information about her birthmother. When Kristen called her, Jo kept referring to Mary Lou as 'Sandra,' which was the name that Allison had given her at birth.

No Time to Wait

Conveniently, Jo lived in a townhouse in south Scottsdale, about fifteen minutes from our office. Because of Jo's advanced age, Kristen didn't want to send paperwork through the mail in case Jo had problems filling in the forms and getting them notarized. She had no idea what Jo's health was like and didn't want to take any chances, so Kristen moved quickly to set up a meeting with Jo as soon as possible. After several phone calls back and forth, Kristen managed to arrange a meeting for 4:00 p.m. the very same day.

Kristen picked Mary Lou up at her home and drove her to Jo's house. When they finally arrived, Mary Lou was directed to stay in the car while Kristen went inside with the mutual consent forms for Jo to sign and Kristen to notarize. Following the letter of the law, Kristen could not allow Mary Lou and Jo to meet before having both parties' signed and notarized consent.

This was a highly unusual way to bring birth families together, but Jo and Mary Lou were eager to meet as soon as possible, and with the paperwork properly completed, and notarized, their reunion could now happen.

Run to Me, Sandra

Mary Lou recalls how her nerves ran wild:

> "I felt like my legs were going to collapse from beneath me. I got out of the car and started walking towards the townhouse when I heard *'Run to me Sandra!'*"

Standing out front waiting was Mary Lou's birth grandmother, Jo—with her arms wide open.

> "I walked right up to her and we hugged for what seemed like an hour. She looked like she'd seen a ghost. 'Oh my darling,' Jo said, tears streaming down her face, 'you look just like your mommy.'"

Kristen watched this scenario play out like a scene from a movie:

> "It was like it was happening in slow motion. Here is this tiny, elderly lady in a print housedress with her little arms stretched wide, hollering for 'Sandra' to run to her. As I stood back near the car, tears rolled down my face as Mary Lou, without hesitation or without even realizing that she was being called 'Sandra' ran into the arms of this smiling old lady."

Mary Lou could see both the joy and the sorrow in Jo's eyes; her daughter Allison should have been there with them. It was a bittersweet celebration, but a celebration none the less. Jo, who was as lively and spry as she could be, gave Kristen some money and sent her to the store to buy a bottle of wine. Kristen took her time on this errand, dilly-dallying at the store, to give Jo and Mary Lou some precious time alone together. When Kristen came back, they all drank a toast to the happy reunion.

The Story of Sandra

Jo and Mary Lou talked for hours. Jo filled her in on her heritage, how her mother, Allison, had become pregnant at the age of 15 as the result of a high school relationship. After 'Sandra' was born, Allison wanted to keep her, and managed to do so for the next nine months. But after much anguish, Allison, her parents and the boy's family all decided the best thing would be to place her in a loving home.

Mary Lou and Jo brought out some family picture albums so that Mary Lou could see the resemblance to her birthmother, and Mary Lou was shocked at how similar their features were. The conversation moved on to Allison's sudden death from a medical oversight nine years earlier, when she was 42 years old. They were both sad that Allison couldn't have been there to enjoy the reunion with them. Jo urged Mary Lou to get in touch with her Aunt June, who was anxious to talk with her as well.

After a four hour visit, Kristen took Mary Lou home so she could share the day's events with Dave and the boys.

Aunt June's Perspective

Two days later Mary Lou called her birth aunt in San Diego. She introduced herself as Mary Lou, a.k.a. 'Sandra.' June was overwhelmed and kept saying, "*Oh my God, oh my God, it's you.*" Mary Lou could feel her aunt's sincerity and conflicting emotions. She knew that simply hearing her voice had upset her aunt. June told her how close she had been to Allison and how her death still affected her. Despite the sad memories it stirred in her, June was thrilled that Mary Lou had found them and that through her, a part of Allison somehow still lived.

To Mary Lou, her aunt was very loving, open and honest. She felt at ease talking to her and have her many questions answered. In just one week, they developed a close and trusting bond. June later sent Mary Lou a package with a letter and photographs of Allison, and also a pair of Allison's earrings and a pendant she had worn until her death.

June was so completely devastated when Allison died that she could not remember how she functioned on a day-to-day basis for the next year. They were extremely close, not just siblings, but best friends. When her mother Jo called to say she'd been contacted by a woman wanting to know if she was interested in meeting Allison's daughter, she urged Jo to meet with her and then have 'Sandra' call her as soon as possible. Here is how June felt after speaking with Mary Lou:

> "To hear her voice was so bittersweet that I just marveled and wept. How could I begin to tell this young woman about her mother, the circumstances of her birth and her placement with her adoptive parents?"

Face to Face with the Facts

Mary Lou flew down to San Diego to meet her aunt. As she came through the airport gate, June grabbed Mary Lou and held on for dear life. June recounted how even though they had already exchanged photos through the mail, the resemblance between Mary Lou and Allison was breathtaking! The rest of the family was scheduled to meet later than evening. June's brother, 'Uncle' Morgan and his wife Jean joined Mary Lou, June, her husband Cam, and daughter Lindsay for an emotional and joyous dinner. When Morgan laid eyes on Mary Lou for the first time, he said, "Well, where have you been for the last 35 years?"

June later told us:

> "My heart was so full of joy, yet filled with sadness, aching that this wonderful reunion was taking place without my sister Allison. She should have been there."

During the two day visit, Mary Lou became very comfortable with all of them. The most poignant part of the reunion was the afternoon the family took Mary Lou to the beach in San Diego where they had scattered Allison's ashes years ago. It felt as though Allison was with them as they sat there on the beach staring out to sea. Mary Lou felt that her mother was looking down on them, and was happy that they had found each other.

The reunion had changed everybody involved. June's words say it all:

> "Many moments were literally surreal to me, truly a life-altering event. I'll never forget that during all of it, the presence of my darling sister was felt so strongly. It was, and still is, incredible."

A New Bond is Formed

June harbored a deep desire for her daughter Lindsay and Mary Lou to become as close as she and Allison had been. She didn't have to worry. When Mary Lou walked off the plane and into her life, Lindsay's first thought was "Oh my God, *yes*." She was the mirror image of her Aunt Allison. Lindsay later related to us:

> "The magnitude of that very moment and the bond we suddenly shared was truly beyond words."

Lindsay came to visit Mary Lou in Phoenix and their bond became even stronger. Mary Lou learned that Lindsay had always been extremely close to her Aunt Allison, who was her friend and mentor as well as her confidant.

Satisfaction at Last

A year after first contact with her birth family, Mary Lou wrote that she was thrilled to report that her relationships with the various members of her new family continued to grow.

Mary Lou was truly fortunate that all of her birth family members were open and honest with their history, with no sense of shame or fear of skeletons in the closet being discovered. Even though she never got to meet her birthmother, finding a loving birth family was the silver lining in her search. She is filled with gratitude for knowing them and is especially thankful for her husband Dave's support and love that provided her with the inspiration to move forward. As she puts it so beautifully:

> "If I had not taken the risk to find them, my life would be remarkably less fulfilled. Each of them makes me feel like I've just returned home from an extended vacation. The truth is, I've always been with them in my heart, but now I'm *really there*."

CHAPTER 14

Jason's Search

The Flower Child

When Jason first contacted us at the end of 2002, we all took an instant liking to him and found him to be a kind-hearted, secure and successful man. He was married with two young sons, and had finally decided to search for his birthparents, hoping at the very least to get medical history. Jason didn't know a whole lot about the circumstances of his adoption, but he did know that the name given to him by his birthmother was 'John Jason.' Because he wasn't adopted until he was nearly five years old, he remembered being in a foster home, and that his adoptive parents visited him there several times before they took him home to live with them.

Jason was born in San Francisco, California in 1970—the height of the hippie era. Because he was born in California, it wasn't difficult for us to determine his birth name and the maiden name of his mother. Our next step was to have Jason write to the county agency that handled his adoption to request his Non-Identifying Information. Fortunately, this particular agency had pages and pages of information regarding his birth and adoption. They gave a copy of the entire file—redacted of course—to Jason. Within that file were the answers to questions Jason had been wondering about all of his life.

The NIDI revealed the sad truth surrounding Jason's birthparents; of tragic lives and circumstances very far removed from the privileged and happy life in which he had been raised.

Jason learned that his birthfather, Devon, and birthmother, Teena, were living together when she got pregnant and, although he was in the process of getting a divorce, Devon was still married to another woman. It was also revealed that Teena had another child, a daughter, Dori, who was in foster care at the time at the time he was born. The truly heartbreaking information was that Teena had been on speed, psychedelics and heroin before, during and after Jason's birth and was a complete addict. She had also been in and out of jail on drug and prostitution charges.

From reading the agency information, it was apparent that Teena had tried to keep Dori in her life by her repeated, and sometimes successful, attempts to get Dori back from foster care during her short periods of sobriety. Teena was clearly focused on trying to keep Dori, but expressed ambivalence about keeping Jason.

Jason was about three weeks old when Teena became so 'strung-out' on drugs that Devon took him away from her, hoping he could keep and care for his son. But, try as he might, Devon just wasn't stable enough to keep Jason. After two weeks, he left him with a couple he knew who lived in another city. Because this couple was not an approved foster care family, Jason was soon removed from their custody and placed in a temporary agency shelter for two months.

A Loving Foster Family

By the time Jason was one year old, he was finally in an approved foster home, where he became extremely attached to his new foster mother. During his time with this foster family, Teena asked about

Jason's welfare just twice and showed only mild interest in visiting him. Eventually, at the firm insistence of the social worker, Teena saw Jason when he was two, but she was very distant with him, and never came back to see him again.

In 1973, abandonment papers were filed on Teena regarding both Jason and Dori. Teena and her attorney met with the county social worker and stated they were going to fight the abandonment proceedings and prevent the adoptions of both of the children. Teena argued that she could be a good mother to both of her children, even though she wasn't sure just how old Jason was at the time. The social worker agreed to put the abandonment on hold for a couple of weeks and left the room for a few minutes to get the necessary papers to file. By the time she returned, Teena's attorney announced that there had been a change of mind and that Teena was ready to place Jason for adoption, but not Dori—she was going ahead with her plan of getting Dori out of foster care and raising her. (Teena's plans would never come to fruition, Dori was subsequently adopted by her foster family and all ties with Teena were severed.)

Going Home with a New Mommy and Daddy

Jason remained with his loving foster family until he was four years old. He had become a happy, well-adjusted little boy. He'd been told he would be getting a new mommy and daddy, but didn't understand that he would have to leave his foster family. The adoptive parents, Marni and Joe, had visited him several times, but when it came time to go home with them, Jason suffered great anxiety.

Jason's foster mother had difficulty facing the separation as well. As they had been together since he was 14 months old, it was as if she was relinquishing her own child. She made the transition as easy as she could for Jason, but on the last day, she fell completely apart, crying her heart out and unable to speak as she handed him over to the social worker.

Although Jason was very unhappy and suffering great anxiety at the separation, he went with the social worker quite readily when the time came. His adoptive parents, Marni and Joe, had visited him previously several times before at the foster home, but now he was a bit apprehensive and shy when he was released to go home with them. He continued to refer to them as 'Mr. and Mrs. Perkins' or 'those guys,' although, within a few weeks he began to call them 'Mommy' and 'Daddy.'

Jason's little life had started off tumultuously, but after his adoption, everything became much more stable. His parents were basically good people, and provided their new son with everything he needed. Surprisingly, Joe and Marni divorced shortly after they adopted Jason, and Marni moved from Los Angeles to San Francisco, leaving Jason totally in Joe's care. However, Marni always kept in contact and visited Jason while he was growing up, and he never felt as if she had deserted him. The circumstances Jason was adopted into were far from ideal, but Jason felt that both his parents gave him everything that they possibly could. He stills maintains a friendly and loyal relationship with both of them.

Consistent with his generous nature, Jason never expressed anger or resentment towards his birthparents Devon and Teena. Quite the opposite, when he learned the details of their sad lives, he felt only pity and sorrow for them. It seemed to us that Jason almost felt 'guilty' for having led a more comfortable life while his birthparents had struggled.

Not wanting to intrude or upset their lives, he asked us to use the utmost sensitivity in contacting Devon and Teena. If we found that either one needed anything, financially or otherwise, Jason said he was ready and able to help. We assured Jason that we always used the utmost discretion and sensitivity in contacting birthparents, and that we would be especially gentle with Teena, whom Jason felt would probably be particularly fragile.

A Visit Home to Two Mothers

Armed with the agency information, it was fairly easy for us to identify and locate his birthparents. We were surprised to find them both still living, considering the hard path they'd followed in the 1970's. Judy found a telephone listing for Teena, still using her maiden name, in a town not far from San Francisco. She called and explained that Teena's birthson, 'John' had asked us to contact her for him. She readily admitted that she was the Teena we were looking for. She had straightened her life out, was single and working as a desk clerk in an upscale hotel. Teena seemed genuinely excited to know that 'John,' now named Jason, was well and thinking of her. She agreed to talk with him over the phone and Judy helped set up the time and date of the phone call. Teena had one more question before Judy hung up: Did Judy know where Dori was?

Jason was happy to hear his birthmother was alive and that she apparently was now living a stable life. They soon spoke on the phone and after catching up on their lives, Teena asked Jason to find his sister Dori for her. He assured her he would try. Then they arranged to meet in person right away. Jason would fly from his home on the East Coast to San Francisco and meet her at a restaurant near the airport.

Jason then called Marni and also made plans to visit her too. He thought that his mom might feel betrayed if she knew about his meeting with his birthmother, so he didn't tell her the real reason he was coming to town.

Within the week, Jason flew to San Francisco. He arrived at the restaurant with flowers in hand, excited and eager to finally meet the woman who gave him life. He waited a long time, but Teena never showed. He finally called her and she told him it was just too much for her, she couldn't go through with the meeting. Dejected, but understanding, Jason went to Marni's for the rest of his time there.

We were all sad that Jason had taken yet another blow from

Teena, but true to his temperament, Jason was accepting and sympathetic. He had even offered to give her money if she needed it. (We love this man).

Progress on the Father Front

While all of this was going on, we were working on locating Devon. After some searching, we identified his ex-wife and through a series of phone calls, we finally reached her. She and Devon had remained on friendly terms since their divorce and kept in touch. She told us that Devon was in poor health and living in a hospice in Montana. They had no private phones in the rooms, but she gave Judy the number for the hospice. Judy called and left a message for Devon to call her back.

Labor of Love

During all of the dramatic events taking place on the East Coast and San Francisco for Jason, we had excitement and worry of our own. Kristen, who was pregnant with her second child, had been hospitalized and then released, but confined to bed rest. As luck would have it, Kristen went into labor right after Judy left the message for Devon to call us!

Kristen insisted she needed Judy in the delivery room with her—in her words, to take care of her husband, who would also be in there. The whole time they were at the hospital, Judy worried and fretted that she would miss the phone call from Devon. Sure enough, Devon did call, but Ava was there to answer and explain the situation to him. She asked him to call back at noon as she was sure Judy would be back by then. Otherwise, he would have to leave a message as Ava was also going to the hospital to be there for the birth of her grandson.

Ava relayed the message to Judy, who then called Jason from the hospital to tell him Devon had called. Jason wanted Judy to be on the phone for a three-way call—he was experiencing a case of the jitters after the incident with Teena. She told him that Kristen was having the baby, but that she would not let him down, she would make it back to the office to receive Devon's call at noon and set up the three-way conversation. Judy felt that Jason had been let down in some way by every mother figure in his life. She knew she couldn't let him down, she had to get that call from Devon—but she also had to be there for her nephew's birth. She was frazzled, running to and fro through the hospital, back to the office (only a mile from the hospital) and making urgent calls from her cell phone. She somehow managed to get through labor and delivery with Kristen, see her new nephew and make it back to the office by noon in time for Devon and Jason's call.

Kristen recalls:

> "I remember Judy talking about Jason and Devon throughout my labor—not that I was really comprehending what she was saying, but she just kept talking, talking, talking about the contact and how Devon was going to call and she had to be there for a three way conversation because Jason was nervous. After an emergency C-section, I remember her hovering over me and tucking the covers around me because I was freezing. Judy, on the other hand was sweating. She kept saying she was sorry that she had to leave me, but I was on enough morphine that I kept saying, 'Go, go! Don't miss that call! But come right back and tell me everything!' I sometimes think we are crazy—even in the midst of an emergency situation, we can't stop working! I find it ironic that even though Judy was the frantic one, running around like an insane person trying to make Jason's dreams come true, I was the one who got the beautiful flower arrangement from Jason—delivered right to my hospital room!"

The Signal

Back at the office for the three-way conversation, Judy spoke with Devon first to explain the reason for her call. Devon was friendly and open. He was very happy to hear that the son he had wanted to keep was looking for him. Devon's first reaction to hearing of the contact with Teena was: "You mean she's still *alive*?!" He explained that when he knew her, she was so badly addicted to drugs that she was near death. He admitted he had been pretty badly addicted himself. Devon was excited to talk with Jason and Judy got him on the phone.

Judy and Jason had agreed that Judy was to stay on the phone as long as Jason needed her to—whether for five minutes or the entire time. When he felt comfortable, he would give her a prearranged signal that she could leave the conversation. About five minutes into the conversation, things were going so well between Devon and Jason, that Jason said, "Judy, don't you think you should be getting back to the hospital to check on Kristen?" That was the signal!

A Final Gift

A few weeks later, Jason called to ask Judy to find his sister, Dori. He wanted to be able to give that to Teena. Judy immediately located Dori, who coincidentally was living only about 10 miles from our office in Arizona. Judy put Dori and Jason in contact. Dori felt tremendous resentment about her life and about Teena, but she was happy that the little brother she remembered contacted her.

She shared details about her early life and the constant upheaval she went through, with short periods of living with her mother and then being placed back into foster care, until she finally was adopted at age ten. She became a very rebellious child and ran away at age 17; she had lived through a lot of hard knocks. As an adult, she was still not quite in control of her life, but had re-established contacts with her adoptive parents and considered them her only family.

Jason urged Dori to call Teena. When she did, Teena was happy beyond belief. It was a testament to Jason's enduring feeling for his birthmother that he pursued this and that he kept in contact with her, and was always kind and considerate. He thought he understood why she did not come to the restaurant to meet him, but the real reason was disclosed a few months later—Teena was not well and didn't want him to know. She passed away just three months after their first contact. Jason was immediately notified, and although Teena had never met her son face-to-face, she had named him the sole beneficiary and executor of her estate. After a lifetime of rejection, she finally let Jason know that he was the most trusted, stable force in her life.

2008 Update

The last few years since the initial search have been exciting and rewarding for Jason. His career has continued to progress, and he and his wife now have one-year-old twin daughters, in addition to their two older sons. After Jason's birthmother's funeral, he contacted Teena's sister, Anne, and then flew to New York City to meet her. He says she is a wonderful and darling person, and he feels she is truly his aunt. Anne says that it is like getting part of her sister back to know Jason, and she is grateful that he somehow obtained stability out of the chaos that he was born into.

After Teena's death, Jason had gone to Montana and spent three days with Devon, just talking and getting to know him. Devon was in a good place in his life at that time, sober and stable, and Jason said he felt lucky that he got to meet him in those circumstances, because shortly afterwards, Devon reverted to his old ways. Jason still keeps in touch with him by phone once in a while, but he does not feel he can include him in his family's lives.

Devon had given Jason the names and addresses of all his other children from previous marriages, and Jason got in touch with most of them. He now maintains close contact with his brother and sister from Devon's second marriage, and feels very close to both of them.

Jason's relationship with his sister Dori is very strained, as she has never straightened her life out and is sometimes incoherent when she calls on the phone once a year or so. Jason has sympathy for her, but says that there is no real feeling of kinship between them.

Jason believes that his search has changed his life completely, and even with the bittersweet knowledge of his parents' turbulent lives, and his unsettled early childhood before adoption, he now has closure in his life. He says he would do it all over again.

CHAPTER 15

Jewell's Search

It's Never Too Late

Many of our searches are done for younger people. Often they have just turned 21 and gained the legal right to search for their birth families. Or maybe they are planning to start a family of their own and want to know their medical histories. So we were particularly touched by Jewell, who was 60 years old when she contacted us.

Older people can be more reluctant to search for their birth families, because their generation holds more of a stigma surrounding adoption and they may be hesitant to reopen old wounds or otherwise 'upset the apple cart.' But as Jewell's search shows, there can be tremendous blessings in having the courage to reconnect at any age.

Jewell was born November 12, 1939, in Muskogee, Oklahoma. Her adoptive mother, Mae, had first heard about her at the town beauty shop, where people were talking about a young woman, Darlene Marks, who was soon to have a third child she couldn't afford to keep. Darlene's two children were already living in her parents' home and she was in the process of divorcing her husband, Earl Marks, who was also Jewell's biological father.

Jewell's adoptive parents jumped at the chance to adopt her. They took her home from the hospital when she was 3-days-old and named her Jewell Sharon Bradford. In February 1940, her adoption was finalized in court, around the same time that Darlene's divorce from Earl was finalized.

Early in 1941, when she was two years old, Jewell's parents packed up and very suddenly left Oklahoma—leaving work and family behind—and moved to California. While it was never said directly, Jewell believed it was because her birth family had come looking for her. With the threat of possibly losing Jewell, her parents chose to relocate.

Jewell always knew she was adopted and was shown her adoption papers more than once growing up. Her parents were very loving and open with her, and she never felt anything but acceptance from them and their entire extended families.

When Jewell was 15, her mother Mae died. At this time, Jewell's father gave her the adoption papers with strict instructions to never lose them. Mae's death was very difficult for both Jewell and her father. She had been the glue of the family. Her father would remarry, but Jewell deeply missed the close relationship with her mother. There were so many things she had wanted to share with her mother, particularly once she married and had daughters of her own.

Growing up, Jewell never had a strong urge to find her birth family. She believes this is because of the warm and secure relationship she had with her parents. After the death of her mother, Jewell began thinking about her birth family, wondering what they were like, but she didn't act on her curiosity. It was never expressed openly, but she felt that her father would have been terribly hurt if she had begun searching.

Exploring Her Past

Jewell married, moved to Ohio and then to Arizona, and raised three children. It was only after her father died, that Jewell began exploring her past. She sent for copies of any papers the Muskogee, Oklahoma Court had on file for Earl and Darlene Marks. She received copies of both of Earl's divorce decrees, one from his first wife and one from Darlene. From these papers she learned the names of her two older siblings, a sister Mara and a brother Christopher. She corresponded with Muskogee County and they sent her copies of both marriage certificates. This gave her a maiden name for Darlene, which was Burton.

Jewell had cancer surgery in 1987 and was encouraged by her doctor to learn more about her family medical history. Still, Jewell didn't pursue her search further until 1999. Then, with renewed curiosity, she began searching the Internet on her office computer at work during her lunch hour. She told her husband about it and he encouraged her to do whatever was in her heart.

Jewell found the Muskogee County Website and began corresponding with a volunteer researcher with the local historical society. This researcher was able to tell her that in the early 40's the Burtons and Darlene Marks had dropped off the tax rolls and phone lists, which meant they no longer lived in Muskogee County, Oklahoma. No clue was left behind as to where they had moved.

Jewell had gone as far as she could on her own. In fact, she'd done very well. When she contacted us and shared the information she'd gathered, we were confident we could help her. Once she gave us the go ahead to search, Jewell recalls that she started trembling because she knew she'd just taken the big step toward actually finding her birth family.

The Hunt for Mara

Since there was no way of knowing if Darlene was still living, we focused our search on Jewell's birth sister, Mara. It didn't take us long to find out that the whole family had moved to the Seattle, Washington area. Judy traced them through the ex-wife of Jewell's birth brother, Christopher, who still lived in the Washington area. Christopher's ex-wife informed her that indeed, Darlene was still alive, gave her Mara's married name and told her where she was living. Before hanging up, she casually mentioned that Darlene had once confided in her that she had placed a baby girl for adoption! It was a leading statement, almost a question of 'is this what you are calling about?' But as shocked as Judy was by her admission, she only replied, 'Really? That's interesting.' She wasn't about to reveal the reason for the call to anyone other than Mara, and we were all excited to have the confirmation that Jewell wasn't a secret to her birth family!

Once we had a work phone number for Mara, it was time to call Jewell and apprise her of our progress. We had great news, but Jewell didn't take it well.

> "I began to shake and cry," Jewell remembers, "I now know that I was afraid of being rejected once again by this family."

After getting Jewell's permission, Kristen made the first contact with Mara on the phone. She explained that she was calling on behalf of a family member. Mara immediately blurted out, *"Oh! It's my little sister, isn't it?"* Her response was so spontaneous and filled with emotion, Kristen had to choke back tears. It seemed like Mara had been on the ready for that phone call for 60 years.

Once she finished talking with Mara, Kristen telephoned Jewell at work. When Jewell heard the news, she immediately called her husband but was crying so hard that she couldn't even talk to him.

That same afternoon, although she could have called Mara, she instead sent her an email. She explains: "I knew I couldn't get two words out over the phone because I'm a crier."

The next day, Jewell finally called Mara. Mara wasn't home at the time, but even just trying to leave a voice mail was too much for Jewell and she started crying again! Jewell composed herself, and she and Mara finally spoke later that same day.

Here's how Jewell describes this emotional time:

> "Over the next several weeks I would start crying for no reason and with no forewarning either. Driving down the road, or at the beauty shop, I had everyone crying with me in happiness, and at church that first Sunday, I was leading the congregational singing—and I broke down again."

Over the next week or so, the emails and pictures flew between the sisters. Jewell learned that she also had a younger half-brother and two younger half-sisters and that her birthmother, Darlene, was still living but suffered from Alzheimer's. She was then 83 years old. Jewell also learned that her birthfather, Earl, had died at an early age in a train accident in San Francisco, California in 1944. Paula, her older half sister, had died the previous year.

An Invitation to a Reunion

Jewell's other siblings soon heard about her and introduced themselves via email. They invited Jewell and her family to a July 4th family gathering in Renton, Washington. Her birthmother, Darlene, would be there, as well as her siblings and however many nieces and nephews could make it.

Jewell's husband thought it was wonderful. But now Jewell was faced with a new challenge—breaking the news to her children. The search had progressed so fast that she hadn't had the chance. Also, she never really imagined she would get concrete results, so she hadn't even mentioned she was searching. Each of her children took the news differently. Her son thought it was great. Her older daughter was in shock and couldn't decide how she felt, and cried several times over the news. Her younger daughter wasn't happy at all; she had a grandpa that could never be replaced and she didn't want another one! But, after being reassured that no one was replacing anyone, she did eventually come around.

So that July, Jewell, her husband and her two daughters flew to Washington to meet Jewell's birth family. Again, even after all the warm communication that had passed between her and her birth family, Jewell still feared rejection:

> "As we pulled up into the long driveway in a rented car and saw all those relatives standing in front of the garage watching, I could have died. If I had been driving, I'd have turned around and left. I have never known such fear! By the time we were parked and unbuckled, my sister Mara was standing at the door. The next few minutes meeting everyone, including my mother who didn't understand who I was, was pretty emotional."

But as the afternoon and evening wore on, Jewell relaxed and began to enjoy visiting her 'new family.' Darlene's sister Bertie was even brought over from a nursing home. She understood who Jewell was and well remembered her sister Darlene 'giving her baby girl away.'

That evening at their hotel, Jewell's family discussed all the similar physical traits and mannerism they'd found between Jewell and her birth siblings. They had plenty to talk about. Since that reunion, the emails have continued to flow between Jewell and her birth family, who have promised to visit her in the Phoenix area.

It's Never Too Late

The reunion was bittersweet for Jewell, since Darlene was not well enough to understand that Jewell was her birthdaughter. But we were thrilled that Jewell finally had the courage to find the people who had been waiting for her so many years. And clearly, Jewell was deeply moved by the experience:

> "The medical information has been valuable, but so has the realization that I am no longer an only child, but surrounded by brothers and sisters. And probably most importantly—the fact that Mara had tried to look for me several times over the years and that they have openly accepted my family and me."

CHAPTER 16

Tim's Search

Right on Time

Tim's story comes partially from Kristen's Confidential Intermediary files and partially from our private investigation files. Tim hired Kristen as his CI in 1998 to find his birthmother, Carol. Nine years later, Tim took the plunge and decided to have our agency locate his birthfather as well.

Tim was born in 1967 and placed with his adoptive parents within a week of his birth. He learned of his adoption only after his mother drowned when he was four years old. Even being raised without a mother, Tim felt no different than other kids. He shared a close relationship with his father Larry, his stepmother and his younger brother, Jeff. Being adopted was simply not an issue for Tim growing up.

When Tim turned 30, he asked his father for a copy of his birth certificate, which he needed for a routine matter. Instead, Larry handed him his adoption papers. His adoption was the last thing on his mind, but he looked the papers over. They piqued his curiosity and he decided to call the agency that had handled his adoption to see if they had information on his birth family. The agency refused to give him any information, so he filed the papers away. But he never forgot about them. He recalls:

> "I became curious about my birth family just before my 32nd birthday. Mainly, I thought it would be good if I knew about any family medical problems which might be in my future. As soon as I made the decision to start looking, the flood gates opened up for me. For 32 years, it was no big deal to me and I guess I didn't want to deal with it. But once I made the decision, I couldn't wait to find out. I was suddenly curious to find out what my birthparents looked like, what they did for a living, what traits I picked up from them and what my life would have been like if I had never been adopted."

While researching how to get more information on his birth parents on the Internet, Tim found the Arizona Confidential Intermediary Program—and Kristen. Tim and Kristen talked extensively over the phone about how the CIP worked. Kristen explained to Tim that if she located his birthmother and she was not open to contact, there could be no exchange of information—either identifying or non-identifying—and the search would be over and the case would be closed. His only recourse would be to have Kristen re-contact his birthmother after one year to see if she had changed her mind. Tim decided this was a risk he was willing to take. He filled out the paperwork and sent it to Kristen.

During their phone conversations, Kristen developed a fondness for Tim. He was full of carefree optimism and told about fun adventures he'd shared with his Dad, his brother and his buddies. In reality, Tim wasn't much younger than she was, but Kristen saw him in her mind's eye as a kid—a kid she really wanted to help. As a mother herself, Kristen felt a pang of sadness for the four year old Tim, who had lost his mother so unexpectedly. She wanted him to at least be able to make contact with a receptive birthmother. Kristen hoped with all her heart that she could help make it happen.

Once the CIP paperwork was approved, Kristen went to the courthouse and reviewed Tim's file. Kristen discovered that Tim's birthmother was Carol Wooten and the file listed her date of birth, address in 1967, and her parents' names. Once back at the office, it was a fairly easy search—Carol had never left the area. Kristen located her whereabouts very quickly, but obtaining Carol's phone number proved to be an impossible task.

Help from A Neighbor

Kristen finally called Carol's next door neighbor and asked her to please get a message to Carol to call regarding a very important matter. Carol called right away and Kristen explained the reason for her call—and immediately assured Carol that she had not divulged anything to her neighbor. Carol was beside herself with excitement. She had waited for this call for many years. As Carol can attest:

> "When I got the call in February of 1999 that Tim was looking for me, I began to sob with joy. God had answered my prayers."

Kristen was extremely relieved that Carol was happy to be found and eager to share herself and her life with Tim. So eager, in fact, that Kristen agreed to go to Carol's office and personally hand deliver the necessary release forms to her the next day. Kristen was taken aback when she met Carol—she was greeted by a warm hug from a stunningly beautiful woman with long, blond curls. Carol generously shared the details of her life as it was in 1966:

> "I was nineteen years old, in my second year of junior college, twenty pounds overweight, had very low self-esteem and was looking to be loved when I found Roger. I met Roger through my brother, who worked with him,

> and because of his acceptance of me, I thought I was in love. My first sexual experience was with him, and as inexperienced as I was, I became pregnant. In 1966, being pregnant was a very humiliating situation to be in and would have been terribly embarrassing for my family had anyone else discovered my pregnancy. I also soon knew that I did not love Roger—nor did I want a child at that time. So, after confiding my situation to my family, Roger and I talked with my parents, and we all made the decision to place the baby for adoption. After that decision was made, it was never mentioned or talked about again in our home until the day Tim and I were reunited
>
> "I stayed at home until a girdle could no longer hide my pregnancy, then I went to the Florence Crittendon Home for Unwed Mothers in Phoenix. I blamed Roger for my situation, as he had assured me I wouldn't get pregnant, and I tried to block everything about him, even his name, out of my memory. Everything about the adoption was very secretive. My parents took care of most of the details and I don't remember a lot. My sister, who is four years younger than me, just recently told me that she had hated me for many years after she learned I was pregnant. I don't recall if I was ever even allowed to make any decisions about the type of family I wanted my baby placed with and I didn't have any curiosity about his adoptive parents. I was never told anything at all about them."

Tim came to our office the next day to hand deliver his release of information forms. He looked much younger than his 32 years, wearing a T-shirt, shorts and sandals. He also bore a striking resemblance to Carol.

Once all the notarized forms were in hand, Kristen called Tim and gave him Carol's home phone number and a time to call. Tim and Carol spoke that very night and discovered that they worked, literally, around the corner from each other. They made plans to meet in person the next day.

An Immediate Bond

Tim and Carol both reported that there was an immediate bond. They became fast friends and Carol soon arranged for Tim to meet the whole family at a gathering. Tim brought two of his friends with him for moral support. Tim expressed that it was a little nerve wracking at first, but soon, he and his extended birth family were having a great time, talking and laughing.

Since Tim and Carol have reunited, they have stayed in close contact and have formed a strong connection. Tim refers to Carol as 'Mom' and Carol refers to Tim as her son. While we find it fairly uncommon for an adoptee to refer to their birthmother as 'Mom,' every circumstance is different. Tim had not had a mother who raised him all of his life, and Carol's strong desire to include Tim in her family as her son made this a natural progression for them. Carol reflects:

> "Tim now being part of the family has strengthened our family—since everything that was once hidden is now known, and there's a peace and an excitement when we are all together. Tim was the missing piece of our family unit. The newness and wonderment of this miracle have worn off, but we've become comfortable together and have a loving closeness that grows as we continue to share our lives with each other."

As Tim sees it, the feeling is mutual:

> "For me, I knew I was going to find my mother. I just didn't expect it to happen as quickly as it did. The search turned out better than I could have ever dreamed. My

> mother has filled a void in my life which I have missed for the last 30 years. She has been a very positive influence in my life. My birth brother and sister have been great and both have welcomed me into the family, as has my grandmother. I see them all often, and after eight years we all have our family routine down for the birthdays and holidays, and it seems to work for everybody."

Tracking Down Roger

Despite his successful reunion with Carol, Tim was not motivated to find his birthfather, knowing it would bother his father, Larry. Larry already had hurt feelings over Tim finding Carol and the close relationship they had formed. Tim never wanted Larry to feel as if he was being replaced. He considered his adoptive family to be his *real* or *first* family. His new relationship with Carol was like finding a long lost relative. Tim says:

> "You are related to them but you don't have the bond you get with growing up with someone."

After Larry passed away in 2005, Tim felt freer to search out his birthfather. He asked Carol about him, but Carol had forgotten or blocked out a lot of the details. Recently, Carol was able to remember some more critical information that was linked to Tim's birthfather. Tim sent the new information to us in an email and asked that we find Roger, and this time to take his case as private investigators.

Because Roger's first and last names were so common, and the surname Carol provided was spelled a bit differently than Roger's actual surname, it was a challenge. Carol was able to recall the name of the street where Roger had once lived. Using an old city directory, we pulled up all residents

living on that street in 1966 and found the true spelling of Roger's last name, as well as a middle initial—a real bonus in our work! Within a week we had located him.

Cautious Contact: Web Site to Web Site

When we first contacted him, Roger was initially cautious, but open to further conversation. We sent Roger a link to Tim's real estate website so he could see a picture of Tim. We wanted Roger to realize that Tim was a stable and successful person, who was not looking for anything other than to let him know that he was alive and well, and to open the door for contact with Roger if he so desired.

We were actually surprised ourselves to see Tim's face on his website after all this time. Since our first meeting, Tim had married, developed his own successful business, and had two young sons. Kristen, upon seeing his current photograph, called Tim and said, "You grew up—you look like a grown man!" He replied, "I guess that's what having kids will do to ya!" Indeed.

Shortly after receiving the link to Tim's website, Roger replied by email, asking us to forward his website information to Tim. He wanted to share with Tim a little bit about his own life through his many career accomplishments.

Now it was Tim's turn to be cautious. We had found Roger so quickly that he was not prepared to start up a fast relationship with him. We offered to act as intermediaries to help facilitate contact between the two men, but Tim decided to email Roger directly and introduce himself. When Tim got Roger's reply, he realized his wife had beaten him to it.

Tim was mortified and a little indignant that his wife would jump the gun and email Roger first, but she just couldn't wait to let Roger know how wonderful Tim is and that his intentions were honest! We had to laugh when Tim told us this story. Wives sometimes love their husbands so much, they can't help but want everyone else in the world to know how great they are. Tim and Roger had a chuckle over it, too, and Roger completely understood.

The Joke's On Us

Roger and Tim agreed to meet for lunch in October, 2007. Afterwards, Tim sent us an email telling us it had turned out awful. Our hearts sank. We continued to read and then, that young kid hiding behind the suit came out and Tim wrote, "JUST KIDDING! It was great!" We sighed with relief. Tim went on to report that they had a nice talk and Tim said it was good to see who Roger was and what he looked like.

Roger has been happily married for many years and has adult children. His wife knew about Tim's existence, but his children did not. He expressed to Tim that he would be sharing the news with them in the future. Tim thought the meeting went well and he feels confident that things will progress at whatever pace is comfortable for both of them.

Ties That Go Beyond Birth

Tim's search has come full circle. He now has the answers to the questions that he waited 40 years for. Meeting Roger was a good experience, but Tim says he definitely experiences a much closer bond with Carol. He feels that part of the reason for this is they were both ready for the connection. Tim says:

> "Timing plays a big role in this stuff...all in all, I'm very happy with the whole experience and I know my mom is thrilled I found her."

Because Tim's story is the last in this book, and because we feel Tim's outlook on his experience may prove inspirational to others, we are compelled to end on this quote from him:

> "I believe that your family (the people who raise you) is where you learn how to love others and that you are supposed to then expand that love to all people you come in contact with. In this way, you come to learn and know you are a part of a higher power or God, and one with each other. I also believe that the love you receive from others comes through them from God and it really doesn't matter, in the big picture, who your family is, adopted or not."

Conclusion

Research Etc. Today

Although Research Etc. has made some changes in the past 13 years, we have retained the same interest, integrity and compassion in our work. We have moved into larger facilities and now have the resources to provide pre-employment screening, litigation research, Civil & Criminal Court records and public record research, in addition to the adoption searches which are still our passion. Judy and Kristen are both Certified Confidential Intermediaries through the Arizona Supreme Court C.I. Program.

In collaboration with Judy's son, Keith Andrews, a Computer Forensics Consultant, we were able to provide additional services such as audio & video tape enhancement, electronic data recovery, NAIS certified email tracing and sensitive document scanning.

Research Etc. is a member of the Scottsdale Chamber of Commerce, the Better Business Bureau of Central/Northern Arizona, BBOnline, and has been a *Registered E-Evidence Partner* with Kroll Ontrack™ since 2004.

Four years ago, we added a new member to our family business with the birth of Rex, who, unlike his big sister Kelsey, did not watch us at work as he played happily in his playpen. On the other hand, he has burped on our computers, filled our fax machine with paper clips, rearranged our files, emptied our desk drawers, papered our walls with pushpins and drawn on the floor with ink. However, although our work load increased, the joy that Rex has brought into our lives is well worth it all—and like we tell our clients, "no use sweatin' the small stuff!"

Adoption Registries & Confidential Intermediary Programs

INTERNATIONAL SOUNDEX REUNION REGISTRY *(ISSR)*

This is a non-profit Mutual Consent Registry founded in 1975 by Emma May Vilardi.

Research Etc. recommends signing up with this trusted agency as the first step in a triad member's search.

P.O. Box 371179
Las Vegas, Nevada 89137
(775) 882-7755 or 888-886-ISRR
www.isrr.net

BIRTHLINE™ REUNION REGISTRY

Research Etc. provides a registry for individuals searching for family members. There is a low one-time setup fee for posting a listing. Searching the site is always free, and several adoptees and family members have been reunited by finding their birth family member's posting on our site.

www.ResearchEtcInc.com

State Programs & Registries

ALABAMA
Search & Consent—C.I.

Search and Consent with Affidavit System for adoptee age 19.
Court appointed intermediary by AA request when no consent on file.
Has a registry; intermediaries may do search via registry filings.

Family Services (Adoptions)
50 Ripley Street
Montgomery, AL 36130

ALASKA
Open Records

Adoptee 18 or older can receive the original birth certificate.
Birth parent can receive names and addresses if there is consent on file.

Family & Youth Services (Adoptions)
PO Box 110630
Juneau, AK 99811-0630

ARIZONA

C.I. Program

The Confidential Intermediary Program certifies and monitors Confidential Intermediaries (CIs) through the Certification and Licensing Division of the Arizona Supreme Court. CIs provide a service to help facilitate contact between parties of an adoption (Adoption triad members) or siblings separated as a result of a dependency action (SIX). Call or email for more information:

(602) 452-3957
(TT) (602) 452-3545
cip@courts.az.gov

Child/Youth/Families Adoptions
PO Box 6123
Phoenix, AZ 85005

ARKANSAS

Adoption Registry

*Agency Registries—C.I.**

*Court order for Confidential Intermediary. Each agency must retain a registry.

Arkansas Mutual Consent Voluntary Adoption Registry
P.O. Box 1437, Slot 808
Little Rock, AR 77203-1437
(501) 682-8462

Child/Family Services (Adoptions)
Div. Social Services Adoptions
PO Box 1437 (Slot 636)
Little Rock, AR 72203
(501) 682-1569

CALIFORNIA

Affidavit System

Adoption Registry

Affidavit system for adoptions finalized after January 1, 1984.
Mutual Consent Program

California Department of Social Services
Adoption Support Unit
744 P Street, MS 3-31
Sacramento, CA 95814

COLORADO

C.I. Program

Adoption Registry

Colorado Confidential Intermediary Services
P.O. Box 260460
Lakewood, CO 80226-0460
(303) 237-6919
Website: *www.cocis.org*

Colorado Voluntary Adoption Registry
Colorado Department of Health
4300 Cherry Creek Drive, South
Denver, CO 80222-1530
(303) 692-2188

CONNECTICUT

Adoption Registry

Agency Registries—Search & Consent

Each agency must maintain a registry. Intermediary Waiver System.

Connecticut Department of Children and Families
Office of Foster and Adoption Services
505 Hudson Street
Hartford, CT 06106
(860) 550-6578
(860) 550-6726 (fax)
http://www.state.ct.us/dcf/foster.htm

DELAWARE
Search & Consent

If birth parents have not filed a veto, adoptees can obtain their original birth certificate at age 21.

Children/Youth/Family (Adoptions)
1825 Faulkland Road
Wilmington, DE 19805

WASHINGTON D.C.
No State Registry

Non Identifying Information at court's discretion.

Dept. Human Health Services/
Adoptions
609 "H" St. NE, 3rd Floor
Washington, DC 20002

FLORIDA
Adoption Registry
Notice & Consent—C.I. *

*if no consent by birth parent then adult adoptee can request a CI to contact birth parent to be advised of the registry.

Florida Adoption Reunion Registry
Florida Department of Health and
Rehabilitation Services
2811-E Industrial Plaza Drive
Tallahassee, FL 32301
(850) 353-0679
(800) 962-3678

Dept. Child/Families/Adoption
1317 Winewood Blvd. #7
Tallahassee, FL 32399-0700

GEORGIA
Adoption Registry
Notice & Consent

Notice and Consent for adult adoptee.

Office of Adoptions
Permanency Support Unit
Attn: Reunion Registry
Suite 13-400
2 Peachtree Street, NW
Atlanta, GA 30303-3142
(404) 657-3559

Dept. Child/Family/Adoptions
2 Peachtree St., NW, 13th Floor
Atlanta, GA 30308
(404) 657-3458

HAWAII
Adoption Registry
Notice & Consent

Notice and Consent for adult adoptee.

Family Court Registry
Court Management Services
777 Punchbowl Street
Honolulu, HI 96811

Dept. Human Services/Adoptions
800 Richards St. Ste 400
Honolulu, HI 96813
(808) 586-5704

IDAHO
State Adoption Registry

Voluntary Adoption Registry
Vital Records Section
Center for Vital Statistics and Health
Policy
450 W. State Street
P.O. Box 83720
Boise, ID 83720-0036
(208) 334-5990
Website: www.state.id.us

ILLINOIS

C.I. Program & Adoption Registry

Confidential Intermediary Service of Illinois
Nancy Golden
3166 Des Plaines River Road Suite 23
Des Plaines, IL 60018
(847) 298-9096

Registry:
Illinois Department of Public Health
Division of Vital Records
Adoption Registry
605 W. Jefferson
Springfield, IL 62702
(217) 782-6553

Children/family Services/Adoptions
405 E. Monroe—# 225
Springfield, IL 52706
(217) 524-2422

Website: *www.idph.state.il.us/vitalrecords/adoptioninfo.htm*

INDIANA

C.I. Program & Adoption Registry

Active registry for those adoptions finalized through December 31, 1993. Court order for confidential intermediary.

Indiana Adoption History Registry
Attn: Registrar, Vital Records Division
P.O. Box 1964
Indianapolis, IN 46206-1964
(317) 383-6280

Department Family/Children/Adoptions
402 W. Washington St.
Indianapolis, IN 46204

IOWA

State Registry, Intermediary System, Affidavit System

Affidavit system for adult adoptee & birth parent. Court Order opens pre June 4, 1941 records

Department Child/Family/Adoption
Hoover State Office Bldg.
Des Moines, IA 50319

KANSAS

Open—Search & Consent

Original Birth Certificate available for adult adoptee. Search and Consent for birth parent, adult adoptee.

Social/Rehab Services
Adoptions
915 SW Harrison—5th Floor
Topeka, KS 66606

KENTUCKY

Adoption Registry

Intermediary System—Search & Consent

Birth Parent consent to release to adult adoptees kept on file.

Program Specialist
Department for Social Services
275 East Main Street
Sixth Floor, West
Frankfort, KY 40621
(502) 564-2147

LOUISIANA

Adoption Registry

Louisiana Adoption Registry
P.O. Box 3318
Baton Rouge, LA 70821
(504) 342-9922
(800) 259-2456

MAINE

Adoption Registry

Open before 1953

Birth Certificates open before September 23, 1953.

Maine State Adoption Reunion Registry
Office of Vital Records
221 State Street
Augusta, ME 04330-0011
(207) 287-3181

MARYLAND

C.I. Program

Adoption Registry

Maryland Mutual Consent Voluntary Adoption Registry
Social Services Administration
Sharon Hackett
311 West Saratoga Street
Baltimore, MD 21201
(410) 767-7372

MASSACHUSETTS

Adoption Registry

Search & Consent

Adoption Search Coordinator
Massachusetts Department of Social Service
24 Farnsworth Street
Boston, MA 02210
(617) 727-0900

MICHIGAN

C.I. Program & Adoption Registry

The Confidential Intermediary Program was established as a court administered program, available through the court for those adoptions in which the former parents' rights were terminated on or after May 28, 1945 and before September 12, 1980.

Department of Human Services
P.O. Box 30037
235 S. Grand Ave.
Lansing, Michigan 48909
Telephone: (517) 373-2035
Fax: (517) 335-6101
TTY: (517) 373-8071

Central Adoption Registry
Michigan Family Independence Agency
Mary Arens
P.O. 30037
Lansing, MI 48909
(517) 373-3513
Written requests only.

MINNESOTA

Search & Consent

*Intermediary System**

*Court order for Confidential Intermediary. Agencies may conduct searches.

Department Children's Services (Adoptions)
444 Lafayette Road
St. Paul, MN 55155

MISSISSIPPI

Adoption Registry

Search & Consent

State may allow search via registry intermediaries.

Department Human Services/ Adoptions
PO Box 352
Jackson, MS 39205

MISSOURI
Adoption Registry
Waiver System

Missouri Division of Family Services
Adoption Information Registry
P.O. Box 88
Jefferson City, MO 65103
(573) 751-3171 or (800) 554-2222

Website: www.dss.state.mo.us

MONTANA
Open—C.I.*

*Court order for Confidential Intermediary.

Adult adoptee can receive original Birth Certificate by written request if their adoption was finalized before 1967. Adult adoptee can receive original Birth Certificate by court order if the adoption was finalized between July 1, 1967 and Sept. 30, 1997. Age of adulthood is 18.

Family Services/ Adoptions
PO Box 8005
Helena, MT 59604

NEBRASKA
State Agency Search
State Registry

Access Veto for adoptions finalized on or after September 1, 1988. Search and Consent for adoptions finalized before September 1, 1988 BP, BR can file affidavits with the Bureau of Vital Statistics.

Rita Krusemark
Division of Children & Family Services
Department of Health and Human Services
P.O. Box 95026
Lincoln, NE 68509-5044
Phone: (402) 471-9254

NEVADA
Adoption Registry
Waiver System

Division of Child and Family Services
Adoption Registry
Capital Complex
711 E. Fifth Street
Carson City, NV 89710-1002

NEW HAMPSHIRE
Open

Adoptee granted access to original birth certificate at age 18 as of January 2005.

Department Child/Families/ Adoptions
129 Pleasant Street
Concord, NH 03301

NEW JERSEY
Private and State Registries
Search & Consent

DYFS of NJ Placements only
Department of Human Services
Division of Youth and Family Services
50 E. State Street
P.O. Box 717
Trenton, NJ 08625
(609) 292-9139

Website: www.state.nj.us/humanservices/adoption/registryframe.html

NEW MEXICO
Waiver System

Court order for Confidential Intermediary

Department of Social Services
Adoptions—Pera Building
PO Drawer 5160
Santa Fe, NM 87502

NEW YORK

Adoption Registry

Agency Registries

Adoption and Medical Information Registry*
Department of Health
Public Health Representative
Corning Tower, Room 208
Albany, NY 12237
(518) 474-9600

*Child must be born and adopted in New York for parties to register. This registry excludes adoptees born in other states and adopted in New York—and the state they are born in may also deny information due to the fact that they were adopted in NY and their records were released to that state.

Child/Family Services/ Adoptions
40 N. Pearl Street
Riverview Center, 6th Floor
Albany, NY 12243

NORTH CAROLINA

Non-ID only

Non-identifying and health history may be released.

Department of Social Services/ Adoptions
325 N. Salisbury
2401 Mail Service Center
Raleigh, NC 27603

NORTH DAKOTA

Search & Consent

Adoption Registry

An agency is allowed to search if the birth parent did not sign a veto.

ND Department of Human Services
Adoption Search/Disclosure
ND Department of Human Services
600 East Boulevard
Bismarck, ND 58505
(701) 328-4805

OHIO

Open & Adoption Registry

The adoptee has access to the original birth certificate if the adoption occurred prior to January 1, 1964.

Ohio Department of Health
Vital Statistics
P.O. Box 15098
Columbus, OH 43215-0098
(614) 644-5635

Dept. Family Services/ Adoptions
65 East State Street, 5th Floor
Columbus, OH 43266

OKLAHOMA

C.I. Program

Adoption Registry

Confidential Intermediary Search Program
Oklahoma Department of Human Services
P.O. Box 25352
Oklahoma City, OK 73125
(405) 521-4373

Voluntary Adoption Reunion Registry
Oklahoma Department of Human Services
P.O. Box 25352
Oklahoma City, OK 73125
(405) 521-4373

OREGON

Open—C.I. Program

Adoption Registry—Agency Registries

Original birth certificate available to adult adoptee.

Oregon State Office for Services to Children and Families
Assisted Search and Registry Program
Permanency and Adoptions Services Unit
HRB, 2nd Floor
South 500 Summer Street, NE
Salem, OR 97310-1017
(503) 945-6643

PENNSYLVANIA
State Registry
Intermediary Waiver System

Allows an agency intermediary to conduct a search. Access to original birth certificate w/ waiver from birth parent.

Adoption Medical History Registry
Hillcrest, Second Floor
P.O. Box 2675
Harrisburg, PA 17105-2675
(717) 772-7015 or (800) 227-0225

RHODE ISLAND
State Registry
Agency release of Non ID Info

Registry:
State of Rhode Island and Providence Plantations
Family Court, Juvenile Division
One Dorrance Plaza
Providence, RI 02903
(401) 277-3352

Child/Family Services/ Adoptions
101 Friendship Street
Providence, RI 02908

SOUTH CAROLINA
C.I. Program & Adoption Registry

South Carolina Department of Social Services
Adoption Reunion Register
P.O. Box 1520
Columbia, SC 29202-1520
(803) 734-6095
(800) 922-2504

SOUTH DAKOTA
Adoption registry

South Dakota Voluntary Registry
700 Governor's Drive
Richard F. Kneip Building
Pierre, SD 57501-2291
(605) 773-3227

TENNESSEE
Open records
State Registry—Waiver System

All records available to adult adoptee upon request. Veto only for adoptees that were products of rape or incest. Contact veto.

Department of Children's Services/ Adoptions
436 Sixth Avenue North
Nashville, TN 37243

TEXAS
State Adoption Registry
Agency Intermediary Service

Central Adoption Registry
Bureau of Vital Statistics
P.O. Box 140123
Austin, TX 78714-0123
(512) 458-7388

Department of Protective Services/ Adoptions
PO Box 149030 (E-558)
Austin, TX 78714

UTAH

State Adoption registry

Utah Department of Health
Vital Statistics
288 North 1460 West
Salt Lake City, UT 84145-0500
(801) 538-6105

Department Social Services/ Adoptions
120 N. 200th West/ PO Box 45500
Salt Lake City, UT 84103

VERMONT

Adoption Registry

Vermont Adoption Registry
103 South Main Street
Waterbury, VT 05671-2401
(802) 241-2122
Website: www.state.vt.us/srs/adoption/registry.html

VIRGINIA

Adoption agency personnel may act as intermediaries.

Confidential Intermediary appointed at adult adoptee's request.

Div. Social Services/ Adoptions
730 E. Broad Street
Richmond, VA 23219

WASHINGTON

Intermediary Waiver System

Washington State utilizes court-appointed Confidential Intermediaries to assist in the search process. For adoptions completed through DSHS and families who adopted a child in state foster care, adoption records are archived through the Children's Administration headquarters office in Olympia.

Dept. Children's Services/ Adoptions
PO Box 45710
Olympia, WA 98504

WEST VIRGINIA

Mutual Consent Voluntary
Adoption Registry

West Virginia Department of Health and Human Services
Office of Social Services
Building 6, Room 850B
State Capital Complex
Charleston, WV 25305
(304) 558-2891

WISCONSIN

Registry
Adoption Records Search Program

Adoption Records Search Program
P.O. Box 8916
Madison, WI 53708-8916
Phone: (608) 266-7163
Website: *http://dhfs.wisconsin.gov/children/adoption*

WYOMING

Intermediary Program

Provides a Confidential Intermediary Program to search for biological family members.

Department of Family Services/ Adoptions
Hathaway Building
2300 Capitol Av., Rm 317
Cheyenne, WY 82001

SpyralSearch™

In 2005, again in collaboration with Keith Andrews, we created a new company, SpyralSearch™ which provides old city directories and telephone books on CD or DVD.

'Spyral' back in time to capture records of people and their lives in past years. Our Directory CD's are easy to use & provide high quality 300 dpi scans of the actual pages in Adobe™ pdf format PLUS—the entire contents are fully text searchable by keywords. These old directories can help you find clues and links to persons and places of a past time period. SpyralSearch™ has made it possible to do research in your own home or office by having the directory information on CD's.

SpyralSearch's website has a complete listing of available directories: www.SpyralSearchSales.com

Order Information for

Back to the Beginning

**Remarkable True Stories of
Adoption Searches and Reunions**

From the Case Files of Research Etc.
Ava Friddle, Judy Andrews, Kristen Hamilton
Private Investigators

With
Joe Bardin

Order on our website:
www.BackToTheBeginningBook.com

Phone Orders:
800-992-3571

Fax Orders:
480-367-0119

Price per copy: $18.95
Arizona Orders: add $1.51 sales tax

Please add $4.00 Shipping/Handling to all orders

Send a check or money order payable to:
Research Etc., Inc.
8390 E. Via De Ventura #F110-184
Scottsdale, AZ 85258-3188

RESEARCH ETC., Inc.
Scottsdale, Arizona